CW00848346

TURNING POINTS

**Changing Your Career
from Science to Patent Law**

DUSTIN T. HOLLOWAY PH.D.

Acknowledgements

I expressly wish to thank all of my colleagues and mentors from the past several years in both science and law. While most of this book was built from my own experiences and studies in patent law, it was still deeply informed by conversations and interactions with many of my colleagues. As with any lengthy project, there are too many people to thank here, but I extend a special thanks to my wife Minita, whose patient conversations and clear insights influence my thoughts and writings everyday. Without her support, this work would have never begun.

Turning Points

1

CHAPTER ONE

Why Intellectual Property Law and Who is this Book For?

Welcome to your journey in search of a new career. Perhaps you are a disaffected graduate student exploring what's out there. Maybe you're an undergraduate engineer looking for next steps. Or maybe you're a post-doc with some experience in patents and you are now ready to take a serious look at intellectual property law. Whatever the case, I hope that we can work through your interests together. The goal of this text is to present interesting alternative career paths for students and professionals in science and engineering disciplines. It is primarily directed toward those pursuing or holding graduate degrees, typically M.S., M.D., or Ph.D. degrees, although much of the information is also applicable to advanced undergraduates in the sciences. In general, the assumed audience is a scientist or engineer having or pursuing an advanced degree.

One motivation for writing this text is my observation that many people invest thousands of dollars and years of studying aimed at becoming an engineer or a scientist, only to discover that life in the lab is not as exciting or glamorous as they expected it to be. Oftentimes in graduate school, the only mentors available to young innovators are professors who have built their entire careers in academia. These mentors are experienced and knowledgeable in their chosen field but frequently coach their students toward academic careers. This should be expected. After all, why would a cancer biologist be inclined to divert his graduate students into law or government policy? Sometimes this bias toward academia exists because the professor feels that a career in academia is the noblest career. They feel that building a life in the pursuit of knowledge and the creation of new technologies is the most important of all career paths. Some scientists may feel that a career in science in the *only* truly worthwhile pursuit! The unfortunate graduate student who studies under such a mentor can look forward to gaining little or no understanding of how their degree can be applied outside of the university.

Regardless of mentorship, graduate programs primarily teach discipline, critical thinking, and technical depth. While this is important, it leaves many students in the lurch, having only the knowledge to apply for technical jobs that they don't find satisfying. Many also feel that it's too late to change careers. Worse, if they do try to leave they may fear criticism from their mentors and colleagues in academia.

Detractors of alternative careers may also be family members who just don't understand the dilemma. After completing a Ph.D. program that may have taken 5 to 7 years (or longer!), how do you explain to your family and friends that you want to take up finance or law? The feared conversation could go something like this:

"Well, dad I've made a decision to go into law."

"What?" he chuckles, assuming you are joking.

You explain, "Yes. I love business and writing, but I just don't like working in the lab anymore. I've looked into this carefully and intellectual property law is perfect for me."

Your father looks confused, and now your confidence is waning. The corners of his mouth turn down, forming that expression you remember from childhood, the one that says, 'You're making another naïve decision.' Finally he speaks, "Why would you change careers after all this work? And after I took that second mortgage to put you through school?! Don't you also want to start a family someday? It's time to be serious about your life."

I hope that this book will convince you not to let fears like these stop you from exploring alternatives. For some, scientific research is a wonderful career. It can offer great satisfaction, especially to someone who loves teaching and the intellectual freedom that the academy offers. However, it is often the case that graduate students, professors, and parents alike don't appreciate the varied possibilities that exist in the world of law and business. If you ever have a conversation like the one above, remind your parent, friend, or spouse that the typical academic post-doctoral scientist makes less than $40,000 per year in the United States. Then point out that *entry level* positions for scientists in law can be as high as $100,000 per year, with salaries increasing to $160,000+ after 5 years.

In the end, one should never make such a huge career change for money alone. A career in intellectual property is demanding and you will have to be interested and passionate in order to be successful. The point of mentioning salary, though, is to emphasize that changing careers does not mean another six years of student loans and microwave noodles. It will be hard work, no doubt, to enter a new field, but you can take part in high-level work and be well paid from the very beginning. Although making a big career change is often a risky venture, a move from science to IP law carries much less risk than you might expect, and law is not as far removed from science as it seems.

From now on, begin thinking of your graduate degree as a ticket. That ticket can take you on several different journeys, not just the traditional rail car to academia. I have tried to write this book as a travel guide to help you understand the career path into intellectual property law, and provide you with the strategies you need to get started with your new job hunt. If nothing else, I hope that this book gives you have a clearer idea about whether patent law is right for you. Happy journeys.

2

CHAPTER TWO

Strife Along the Beaten Path

A graduate student in science/engineering typically has two career paths available: academia and industry. Although this orthodoxy is deeply ingrained in the scientific culture, it has begun to change in recent years. The pressures of globalization and the need to innovate have created a demand for highly skilled professionals in a diversity of nontraditional fields. Nevertheless, it is important to understand the usual options to fully appreciate why some scientists grow frustrated with them. In this chapter we will briefly review academia and industry with a particular focus on what drives people to start looking at alternatives.

Academia

To anyone studying for an advanced degree, the academic track is an obvious one. After a Ph.D., many graduates apply for a post-doctoral position, often to do work similar to their Ph.D. studies (but for slightly higher pay). As a post-doc you are more senior than graduate students and, if you're lucky, you can apply for and win grant money to conduct your own research. This can be exciting and rewarding, especially if you are passionate about research. In some of the best (*i.e.,* well funded) institutions, there may be increased flexibility to pursue interests apart from those of your supervisor. On the other hand, grants are hard to win, and it can be difficult to pursue your own research agenda while still fulfilling the expectations of your boss.

After a few years as a post-doc, typically 4 to 7, you can apply for faculty positions.[1] If you are lucky enough to land a faculty level job, you face a new set of challenges. Winning grant money and regularly publishing will be the most prevalent obstacles you face while working to convince senior faculty that you are worthy of tenure. You won't typically expect to achieve tenure until you are about forty years old, but this can, of course, vary widely from person to person. Nevertheless, once you have tenure you will enjoy a job that is, for the most part, guaranteed for life. Aside from your teaching obligations, you will then be free to direct your research however you please. From this perspective, being a university professor can be one of the most rewarding and satisfying jobs imaginable. Who wouldn't want to follow their interests, set their own hours, and enjoy a high level of respect?

But life isn't so simple. Good post-doctoral positions are difficult to come by and often have narrow pre-requisites (do you have a foundation in quantitative neuroscience, skills in micro-array analysis, understanding of multi-variate statistics, and knowledge of cell-culture methods?). Most of the time you'll end up following your professor's orders, with little time left over for your own research pursuits. Many post-docs can end up spending six to ten years completing different projects in an attempt to build a research story that can help them land a faculty level job. This is a daunting prospect considering that the typical post-doctoral salary is around $45k/year... hardly enough to support a family if you live in a major metropolitan area. Also, tenure track jobs are competitive and very difficult to come by, and paper qualifications tend to be more important than many would like

---

1 This timeline is typical if you expect to work in the life sciences in a research university. A post-doctoral position may not be required at all if you are interested in a teaching position at a regional school.

to admit (Do you have a 4.0? Are you from Harvard? Did you publish in Science or Nature?). If you want to be a professor in a hot market like Massachusetts, New York, or California, it could be easier to spot Sasquatch than win a tenure track position.

Ok, I exaggerate a little. But the truth is that the academic track is wrought with politics, low pay, stiff competition for funding, and, in some markets, a dearth of opportunities. Post-docs are the workhorses of science, doing most of the heavy lifting and getting the least compensation. All the while, the tasty carrot of tenure is hanging out in front, very, very far in the future. To choose this career path requires persistence, deep passion, and a true love of scientific pursuit.

Industry

For those frustrated with academia, industry offers a possible alternative. A career with a pharmaceutical company or a smaller biotech can offer higher pay and regular work hours, but the tradeoff is that there is much less opportunity to pursue your own passions in science.

At a company you must follow the research goal of your employer. For some, this is the perfect recipe for happiness. Industry offers cutting-edge science, freedom from grant applications, and a higher salary. For others, however, this arrangement takes away the excitement. Depending on the company, a scientist at a pharmaceutical firm may feel like little more than a glorified lab technician, performing the same experiments over and over while the upper management makes the key decisions about research priorities. One also has to remember that any knowledge created while working for a company is proprietary. Although a scientist in industry may be an "inventor" of a particular piece of science, it is generally the company that holds rights to any technology developed or patents filed. If you give up your industry job, you will not be able to share the details of your work with anyone else or leverage the systems you developed to aid you at a new job. As an employee, you have to accept the fact that you are being paid for a service: the glory of scientific creation is not yours to exploit.

And, of course, the motivations of a company are very different than an academic lab. At a company you may not be free to publish in the same way you would be at a university. You may also find that the chief concern of your managers is the market position of a scientific product (*e.g.*, drug or instrument) rather than the altruistic goal of improving the human condition.

Finally, although the salary is better in industry, there is typically an upper limit to possible earnings. Certainly with the right maneuvering, it is possible to eventually leave the lab, join management, and spend more time directing science departments. Barring that, however, the typical industry scientist will start at a salary of about $50-$90k/year and struggle to earn beyond $150-$170k/year during the course of their career. Although truly respectable, those figures pale in comparison to the $160k/year *starting* salary that some attorneys make at big firms.

Other Frustrations Along the Beaten Path, and a Way Forward

Sometimes, after enduring the rigors and frustrations of graduate school, it is just unthinkable to continue doing scientific research any longer. One of the most common complaints about graduate life in academic research is that a scientist's exposure to science is too narrow. When someone hears a scientist complain that he doesn't see enough science, it sounds absurd! But, the problem is that the more research you do and the more expert you become, the more focused your area of expertise. In the beginning you study biology, then perhaps mammalian vascular biology, and later the oxygen dynamics of bovine lung cells. For someone who loves science in general, it is a disappointing realization that a scientist can become more detached from the broader arena of cutting edge science as they become increasingly specialized and expert in one particular niche.

In summary, difficulties along the "beaten path" of academia and industry can include low pay, unsatisfying work, a narrow exposure to science, difficulty in obtaining funding and lack of control over career direction. All careers have their drawbacks and all have their perks, but if these factors have led you to conclude that scientific research is no longer in your future, know that you are not alone. Other career options are available, and scientists are well positioned to succeed in alternative careers like law and business.

3

CHAPTER THREE

Patent Law: An Overview

In order to fully explore Intellectual Property (IP) law as career option, it is first necessary to discuss the essentials of the field. I don't intend to teach the specifics of the law here; I only wish to orient the reader to the subject. This will help in building a more realistic picture of the day-to-day curricula of a job in patent law.

IP law is simply the area of law dealing with intangible property: ideas, inventions, concepts, designs, symbols, etc. An intellectual property lawyer is charged with protecting, establishing, and managing this property for their client. As a subject area, IP law encompasses at least three primary areas of specialty: patents, copyrights, and trademarks.

Many people are more familiar with copyrights and trademarks than they are with patents. Copyrights are the legal protections that artists and authors receive on their written or recorded work (think of a novel or a music album). Trademarks are perhaps the most familiar because they surround us every day. The famous red swoosh of Coca-Cola™ and the ubiquitous Intel Inside™ logo are both good examples of official product trademarks. Companies use trademarks as symbols for their products or brands, and these symbols can be extraordinarily valuable in building a consumer following.

In order to work with copyrights and trademarks it is necessary to have a J.D. degree, so it is unusual for a scientist or engineer to have any exposure to these types of intellectual property during the first 4 or 5 years of working in the profession. As such, patents are the bread and butter of a new recruit in an IP-law firm.

According to the United States Patent and Trademark Office (the USPTO) website:

> "[a] patent for an invention is the grant of a property right to the inventor, issued by the United States Patent and Trademark Office...The right conferred by the patent grant is, in the language of the statute and of the grant itself, 'the right to exclude others from making, using, offering for sale, or selling' the invention in the United States or 'importing' the invention into the United States."[2]

The grant of a patent on an invention makes the ownership of that invention just as real as the ownership of a tract of land or an article of clothing. The owner of a patent can prevent others from using his invention or demand that they pay a fee for its use (*i.e.*, a royalty or license fee). The owner may also completely sell the rights to his invention for a negotiated price. In today's world of high technology, patents are of paramount importance. For example, a drug company may spend $1 billion to develop and test a new drug. Such a big investment is hardly worthwhile if one of their competitors can simply copy the drug and sell it at a cheaper price. A patent allows the innovator to maintain exclusive control over his invention, and literally dominate the market for the term of the patent. This benefits society by: 1) rewarding inventors for their hard work, and 2) encouraging companies and individuals to spend time and money developing technology. Indeed, it is often the case that it would not be worthwhile to invest so much money to develop a new technology if you could not exclusively exploit the results.

Exclusive control and ownership is a strong incentive for technological innovation, and companies demand that their legal representatives

---

2 United States Patent and Trademark Office, "Information Concerning Patents," http://www.uspto.gov/patents/resources/general_info_concerning_patents.jsp [accessed July 28, 2011].

have a solid understanding of the science at issue. For this reason, law firms are increasingly hiring engineers and Ph.D.s to bolster their capacity to handle scientifically intense patent applications and litigation issues. Indeed, many of the top partners in the field are doctors or engineers.

Box 3-1 provides a summary of the types of patents available in the United States. Since Utility patents are the primary vehicles for protecting the scientific innovations of science, they will be the focus of our discussions in this book.

Box 3-1 Three Types of patents in the US[3]

1) Utility patents- This is the most common type of patent and practically the only one that a scientist will come across during his initial years in the field. A utility patent may be granted for an invention that is a "process, machine, article of manufacture, or composition of matter, or any new and useful improvement thereof." 35 U.S.C. §101

2) Design patents- Patents granted to ornamental designs. As an example of this, think of the latest sneaker design, a sleek new bathroom faucet, or the look of the new iPod. The patent is not directed to the technology, but to the appearance and distinct "look" of the article;

3 For Utility Patents see: Legal Information Institute. "U.S. Code." Cornel University Law School. http://www.law.cornell.edu/uscode/35/usc_sec_35_00000101----000-.html [accessed August 1, 2011]
For Design Patents see: Legal Information Institute. "U.S. Code." Cornel University Law School. http://www.law.cornell.edu/uscode/35/usc_sec_35_00000171----000-.html [accessed August 1, 2011]
For Plant Patents see: Legal Information Institute. "U.S. Code." Cornel University Law School. http://www.law.cornell.edu/uscode/35/usc_sec_35_00000161----000-.html [accessed August 1, 2011]

> 3) Plant patents- Granted for new asexually reproduc-
> ing plants. Certain types of plants, such as tuber prop-
> agated plants or plants found in an uncultivated state
> cannot be patented (see 35 U.S.C. §161). Examples of
> tuber-propagated plants are, according to the MPEP,
> the Irish potato, and the Jerusalem artichoke.

Patent law in the United States is written under Title 35 of the United States Code[4] (Abbreviated as "35 U.S.C."). Title 35 is statutory law enacted by Congress and represents the highest authority on matters of intellectual property (as related to patents). Congress has also bestowed rulemaking authority to the United States Patent and Trademark Office. Rules created by the PTO are collected in the Code of Federal Regulations or "the CFR" for short. The CFR does not hold the weight of statutory law, but is used to set out the procedural rules that must be followed during the filing, examination, and general prosecution of patents.

The PTO has also compiled a very useful guidebook called the Manual for Patent Examining Procedure, commonly called the MPEP. The MPEP brings together the relevant laws and rules, along with coherent explanations that describe how a patent should be filed, what it should include, how it should be evaluated, and how practitioners should conduct themselves as they prosecute patents at the PTO. As the name suggests, the MPEP serves as a manual for Patent Examiners, and describes how they should examine and critique a new application. The MPEP is so central to practicing patent law that it is the foundation for the Patent Bar Exam, which is the qualifying exam required for officially practicing before the PTO.

Sometimes it can be confusing for patent law newcomers to understand where to look for information. Generally, the first stop in the search for any answer is the MPEP, because it will restate the law (Title 35) and the Rules (CFR) and even explain critical case law within the convenient framework of a user manual. Because the MPEP is so large,

---

4 Legal Information Institute. "U.S. Code." Cornel University Law School. http://www.law.cornell.edu/uscode/35/ [accessed July 28, 2011]

the best place to begin is its index. Learning how to quickly find the right subject in the index of the MPEP can save a considerable amount of time. Indeed, this skill is absolutely vital to passing the Patent Bar Exam and necessary for finding the answers to questions that come up during the day-to-day work of patent practice.

In the next section we will look briefly at the scope of patents in the U.S. and the tests that an invention must pass in order to be patented. As a brief overview, the idea or invention must first be shown to fall under what is considered "patentable subject matter." Once this hurdle is passed, an invention must then be determined to be novel, and non-obvious. We will now discuss each of these criteria in turn.

Patentable Subject Matter

The first question that comes to mind when beginning patent law is: What is patentable? What are the limits of patentability? Can an idea be patented? A mathematical formula? What about the discovery of a new species or animal?

The law regarding what is patentable is set forth in 35 U.S.C. sec 101:

> Whoever invents or discovers any new and useful process, machine, manufacture, or composition of matter, or any new and useful improvement thereof, may obtain a patent therefor, subject to the conditions and requirements of this title. [5]

Simply looking at the law above would suggest that essentially anything that is new and useful is patentable. This is not the case in reality, primarily because the courts have more narrowly construed the law.

To fully understand how a court can interpret a law, we need to briefly discuss the difference between common law and statutory law.

---

5 Legal Information Institute. "U.S. Code." Cornel University Law School. http://www.law.cornell.edu/uscode/35/usc_sec_35_00000101----000-.html {accessed August 1, 2011}

Up to now we have only seen the laws passed by Congress (the U.S.C.) and the Rules promulgated by the PTO (the CFR), but the law created by judges in the course of hearing and deciding cases colors all aspects of IP law. Judge created law, or "common law," is the law fashioned in the courts as judges attempt to apply the statutes to specific and complex issues. The courts are not actually inventing new law here, but deciding how best to *interpret* the laws created by Congress. This kind of legal system is used widely throughout the world, and most countries (including the U.S.) inherited the common law traditions from the United Kingdom. Such common law has a significant impact on all aspects of patent law. In the case of sec 101, the courts have held, for example, that abstract mental processes and laws of nature (even if newly discovered) are not patentable. This makes perfect sense, because it would be fundamentally unfair (not to mention silly) to allow people who discover a natural law to patent it. Einstein's $E=mc^2$ is a good example of a natural law. It describes a natural relationship between matter and energy that is inherent to the universe. However, there is no reason why someone couldn't use Einstein's principle to develop a new technology or machine that may be patentable. So, while Einstein's equations are not patentable matter, a nuclear reactor based on those principles might be a patentable device.

Novelty

In order for an invention to be patentable it must also be novel. Put simply, this means that someone else must not have previously invented it. The relevant language for this test of patentability is found in 35 U.S.C. sec. 102. Although this sounds like a common-sense test, it has many complex intricacies. For instance, what would it mean to be previously invented? What if, before I invent a new kind of doorknob, a Tibetan monk actually conceived of the same high tech knob, but only produces it after I file my doorknob patent? Is his idea, occurring far away in the Tibetan mountains, enough to prevent me from patenting my doorknob, even if the monk never tells anyone of his secret creation? And, what if I put my doorknob in a poster presentation before filing the patent? Can my own disclosure be used against me?

You can easily see that the concept of novelty can become very complex depending upon where the limits of disclosure, conception, and reduction to practice are drawn. The answers to the questions above are explained in detail in the MPEP and any scientist or engineer entering into the field will spend a considerable amount of time studying these issues during their first year at a firm. Though it is beyond the scope of this book to delve so deeply into the law of novelty, my point here is that the underlying issues are far more complex than they initially appear. For the interested reader, a link to the full text of section 102(a)-(e) is given in a footnote below[6].

Obviousness

Just as with novelty, the issue of whether an invention is obvious or not may require a complex investigation. In order to make this determination, the law creates an imaginary figure, the "skilled artisan," to serve as a standard of comparison. The skilled artisan for any particular invention is simply a knowledgeable practitioner in the field related to the invention. If the invention is a new kind of elevator, then the skilled artisan might be thought of as an engineer involved in elevator design. If the invention is a new cancer drug, then the skilled artisan may be conceived to be an oncologist or a research scientist. Keep in mind that the "skilled artisan" does not necessarily encompass the prodigy expert at the top of the field[7], but rather the average, highly knowledgeable practitioner.

The question of obviousness, then, centers on whether the invention would have been obvious to such a skilled artisan at the time the patent was filed. If the PTO determines that the invention would have been obvious to that person, then the invention is unpatentable.

Upon first learning of the application of obviousness in patent law, it is natural to wonder how a Patent Examiner or a court could

---

6 See: http://www.uspto.gov/web/offices/pac/mpep/documents/
appxl_35_U_S_C_102.htm
7 The reason for this is that most things would, arguably, be obvious to such a genius.

objectively determine whether highly complex inventions are obvious or not. In truth, obviousness decisions are wrought with difficulties, and the law is continually being reviewed and revised in the courts. For the patent practitioner, the challenge is to remain abreast of the current interpretation of the law so that you can make the best arguments for your client.

The Parts of A Patent and How they are Written

Patent writing typically begins when an attorney or agent receives a technology disclosure from an inventor. In some cases this disclosure is well developed and detailed, containing many pages of text, data, and figures. In other cases, the disclosure consists of as little as a few paragraphs of ideas with some preliminary results, carving out an inventive concept.

In either case the attorney (or patent agent) will study the subject matter carefully and begin writing. The writing process, even under a tight deadline, will generally consist of several full document revisions that are sent back and forth between the inventors and the attorney. Particular attention must be paid to getting specific and accurate language into the claims, which is the part of the patent that legally embodies the invention to be patented[8].

Altogether, a patent consists of roughly 7 parts: Title, Abstract, Background, Summary, Detailed Description, Examples, and Claims. Though the Title and Abstract will be familiar to anyone who as written or read a scientific journal, the other sections merit some brief discussion. The Background section of the patent describes the problem to be solved by the invention. Although it is similar to the background

---

8 It may be useful to look at a few patents online to get an idea of the work product created by the patent writer. One simple way to check out a few patents is to do a term search on Google Patent (choose some specific terms that are of interest in your field, e.g., "DNA," "antibody," or "integrated circuit.").

section of a science article such that it provides an overview of the state of the art, the patent writer must take additional time to describe the unmet needs of current technology or the deficiencies in the current methods. This serves the crucial purpose of focusing the reader on how the present invention is a solution to known problems or is an inventive leap over previous technology. Since a good attorney will anticipate that the Patent Office may reject the claims for reasons of obviousness, this is a good place to set up the later argument that the invention is clearly new and non-obvious.

The *Abstract* of the patent is supposed to succinctly outline the invention. When attorneys search for patents in databases, it is quite often the titles and abstracts which are searched for key words. Because of this the Abstract should contain the key words and ideas that fit the invention most closely. In reality, however, some patent writers are purposely obtuse in their language in an attempt to prevent the document from being discovered easily in simple subject searches. Nonetheless, good abstract writers are as clear as possible.

The *Summary* section is a set of statements which lay out the bare basics of the invention more specifically than the abstract. The summary is longer and isn't bound, as the abstract is, with a 250-word limit. Typically, the summary is an expanded restatement of the patent claims in paragraph form. Accordingly, the summary is written only after the claims are finalized.

The *Detailed Description* is generally the largest part of the patent and teaches each and every aspect of the invention in as much detail as possible. For example, suppose your particular invention is a special gene that makes hamsters glow in the dark. In the detailed description you should describe the gene, provide its DNA sequence, discuss how you produce the DNA, how you transfer the DNA into the hamster, and exactly how you ensure that the hamster glows at the right times and in the right bodily tissues. You will want to describe all of the tools, protocols, and instruments you used, as well as alternatives that may achieve the same result. Essentially, whatever the invention is, the Detailed Description should provide such information that a skilled artisan would understand that the inventor was in possession of the invention at the time the patent was filed, and further provide enough detail for a skilled artisan to make and use the claimed invention[9].

The Detailed Description further includes and *Examples* section. Ideally, the examples describe how the invention was reduced to practice. Each example may describe a specific scientific protocol or set of results

---

9 35 U.S.C. §112: "The specification shall contain a written description of the invention, and of the manner and process of making and using it, in such full, clear, concise, and exact terms as to enable any person skilled in the art to which it pertains, or with which it is most nearly connected, to make and use the same, and shall set forth the best mode contemplated by the inventor of carrying out his invention.

The specification shall conclude with one or more claims particularly pointing out and distinctly claiming the subject matter which the applicant regards as his invention.

A claim may be written in independent or, if the nature of the case admits, in dependent or multiple dependent form.

Subject to the following paragraph, a claim in dependent form shall contain a reference to a claim previously set forth and then specify a further limitation of the subject matter claimed. A claim in dependent form shall be construed to incorporate by reference all the limitations of the claim to which it refers.

A claim in multiple dependent form shall contain a reference, in the alternative only, to more than one claim previously set forth and then specify a further limitation of the subject matter claimed. A multiple dependent claim shall not serve as a basis for any other multiple dependent claim. A multiple dependent claim shall be construed to incorporate by reference all the limitations of the particular claim in relation to which it is being considered.

An element in a claim for a combination may be expressed as a means or step for performing a specified function without the recital of structure, material, or acts in support thereof, and such claim shall be construed to cover the corresponding structure, material, or acts described in the specification and equivalents thereof." Above text taken from: The United States Patent and Trademark Office, Manual for Patent Examining Procedure 35 U.S.C. §112, http://www.uspto.gov/web/offices/pac/mpep/documents/appxl_35_U_S_C_112.htm {accessed August 1, 2011}

obtained, showing that each piece of the invention works. An example may also be what they call "prophetic." A prophetic example, rather than describing experiments that have already been performed, instead describes experiments that may be carried out in the future. Such prophetic examples are also accompanied by a discussion of the expected results. Generally speaking, if an inventor brings a fully fleshed out scientific paper to an attorney, the specific procedures, tables, and figures of the paper often end up being worked into the example section of a patent. Experiments that are instructive to describe, but have not been performed, may be written into the patent application as "prophetic" examples. Such examples serve to illustrate results that are considered expected or obvious, or show alternative methods to arrive at the invention.

Finally, we come to the *Claims* of the patent. The claims are the most important part of the document. Although a great deal of time is spent on the patent Description and Examples, it is the Claims that actually define the boundaries of the invention. When a patent is challenged in court, or when someone is accused of infringement it is the wording and construction of the claims that are analyzed to determine the scope of the invention and the true breadth of what the patent holder "owns." Because they are so important, a disproportionate amount of time is spent on drafting the claims in very specific and creative ways. Usually, the claims section is the first thing to be written once the attorney fully understands the invention. After the claims are complete and agreed upon with the inventors, the remainder of the patent document is written with an emphasis on supporting and illustrating the claims. Claim drafting is as much art as science and the skill can take years to fully master. Most law schools with any emphasis on intellectual property will offer full courses dedicated entirely to drafting patent claims.

Types of Work: Patent Prosecution

There is no question that mastering the basics of patent prosecution is an intimidating and humbling experience, especially for a professional such as an engineer or a Ph.D. who is arguably a expert of his or her respective field. Whatever your feelings on the matter, just realize that it is relatively common for newcomers with technical backgrounds to have an almost complete ignorance of patent law when they join their first law firm. Some firms will provide training programs to get new hires up to speed while other firms prefer them to begin work immediately and learn through interactions with partners and associates. The key to survival in either case is to be assertive about asking questions, however basic, and get comfortable with searching for answers in the MPEP.

Appendix A provides a short list of resources to begin your first explorations and study of patent law (hopefully before you go to your first interview!). I've said that many scientists join firms with no background in law; however, if you can demonstrate interest in and knowledge of the key aspects of patent law, this could be a huge advantage in your job hunt.

Typically, a scientist who enters patent law will spend the majority of their time writing patents, preparing arguments against an Examiner's rejections, or preparing letters of instruction to foreign attorneys to argue against Examiners in foreign countries (more on international prosecution later). This section on prosecution will focus on the primary task of examination before a patent examiner.

Once the patent document is written to the client's satisfaction, the agent will file it as a patent application with the PTO. At this point, as long as the application contains all of the necessary elements and documents, and if it truly encompasses only a single invention, the PTO will assign the application to an Examiner, thus beginning the prosecution phase. Patent prosecution is the process of defending a patent application before the PTO, and trying to convince an Examiner that particular claims should be upheld or that certain claim language should be allowed. It may also involve more complex tasks, such as working through a Reexamination, Interference, or other proceedings where a patent application is challenged outside of court.

The Examiner assigned to the case will conduct a search in technical journals, databases, etc. to find information that may render the claims unpatentable. If the Examiner finds such information (called "prior art") they will write a report called an Office Action, describing their findings and rejecting specific claims in the application. For example, the Examiner might say, "Claims 1-3, 6, 9, and 18 are rejected under 35 U.S.C. sec 102(a) as being anticipated by Smith *et al.*, US. Patent No. 1234567 who states that…"

Once the Examiner has issued such a rejection it becomes the agent's responsibility to review the references cited by the Examiner, suggest amendments to render the claims patentable, and/or prepare arguments to persuade the Examiner to reconsider the rejection. This may also require considerable interaction with the inventors and licensees as they weigh in on potential amendments and the merits of the cited art. At this stage, input from the inventors can be particularly important in demonstrating that the technology was novel and inventive at the time of filing.

Responding to Office Actions requires intensive study of the subject technology and can sometimes be one of the most rewarding aspects of patent law. An intelligent and focused attorney with a solid grasp of science can take great pride in winning a patent with valuable claims for their clients. Aside from the clear economic benefits to the client, successfully making complex arguments rooted in science and law can be both satisfying and intellectually exciting.

This back-and-forth with the Examiner may continue for several iterations as the claims are amended and arguments considered. If the prosecution reaches an impasse where the Examiner makes a final holding that the claims are not patentable, the applicants may choose to abandon the application, file an alternative application (or something called a "request for continued examination"), or file an appeal to the Board of Patent Appeals and Interferences (BPAI)[10]. More commonly, the applicants and the Examiner will reach a consensus on a set of claims that are allowable, and the application will proceed to issuance as a patent.

Although the preparation of arguments and claim amendments is a substantial part of patent prosecution, a variety of other types of work is also available. For example, inventors will provide various types of data and figures in support of a patent and those figures have to be properly formatted and submitted according to certain specifications. Some firms employ a draftsman for this purpose, but the patent practitioner will have to direct and correspond with the draftsman. A similar situation arises when biological sequences (*e.g.*, DNA or protein) are

---

10 Be aware that these procedures are always subject to change. As of the date of this writing, Congress is considering changes to U.S. Patent Law which could drastically alter the way prosecution is conducted.

submitted with a patent application. Detailed sequence listings must be prepared and firms vary on whether they prefer patent agents, outside consultants, or specialist paralegals to handle this work. Other elements of prosecution, which we won't discuss further, are preparation of declarations by the inventors, preparation of assignment documents, correcting errors in patent applications, preparing arguments and submissions for interference proceedings and reexaminations, and preparing appeal briefs when the applicant decides to appeal the decision of an Examiner.

While U.S. prosecution is often the "bread and butter" of any patent attorney, international prosecution is becoming ever more important as companies seek to bring their products to overseas markets. The next section spends some time discussing the importance of international patent work.

Some Notes on International Prosecution

It may come as a surprise that a substantial portion of your work will involve prosecuting patents internationally. Applicants filing a patent application in the U.S. have a limited time in which to decide whether they wish to protect their technology in the United States only, or if they wish to extend that protection to other countries.

In a common scenario, the first document to be filed is a "provisional U.S. application." The provisional application is essentially a placeholder that establishes a filing date for the patent (which is *very* important for determining what constitutes prior art). The filing of a provisional does not start the patent term running, nor does it initiate examination[11].

At the end of 1-year, the Applicant must decide whether they wish to file only a U.S. patent application or if they wish to file an international application (also called a PCT application, named after the international treaty which created it, the Patent Cooperation Treaty). The PCT application is essentially another kind of placeholder, which exists

<hr>

11 Note that Applicants do not have to file a provisional at all. They may proceed directly to filing a full patent application or an international application. In practice, most people choose to file a provisional application first.

until the application is transmitted to national patent offices. The advantage of the PCT application is that it provides a single vehicle and a single format by which an applicant can submit his application to every nation that has ratified the Patent Cooperation Treaty. As of 2009, there are 142 countries that have contracted to the PCT. Unlike the U.S. provisional application, a PCT application undergoes a partial examination process whereby it is evaluated according to the standards of novelty, obviousness, and clarity. The Examiner will establish a search report and Written Opinion as to the patentability of the invention, and these results will be shared with all of the national patent offices. This initial set of search results can save the applicant considerable time since they establish a common set of issues which will likely come up during examination in each PCT country (though national offices are by no means limited to the issues raised by the PCT Examiner).

The bulk of international patent prosecution begins once a PCT application is disseminated to the national offices. A patent practitioner must then correspond with attorneys in each foreign jurisdiction, providing instructions on how to respond to Office Actions in each member country. The foreign attorneys will often be relied upon to explain the intricacies of patent law in their home countries and further suggest strategies for responding.

One can now begin to appreciate the complexities of international patent practice. A single U.S. invention may require independent prosecution in many countries, requiring correspondence with attorneys in Europe, Japan, Australia, India, New Zealand, South Africa, China, etc. Each country will also have its own rules on patent ownership and assignments, and will further require the docketing and organization of deadlines specific to that country. Despite the seeming complexities, the international patent application process has been greatly simplified by the PCT, since it is not necessary to make independent country applications throughout the world. Indeed, the World Intellectual Property Organization has noted that the number of PCT applications has been growing rapidly, especially in recent years. The figure below further illustrates the substantial increases seen in PCT application filings since the mid 1990s. Considering the trends, learning international prosecution is unavoidable for any practitioner who wishes to advance their career in patent law.

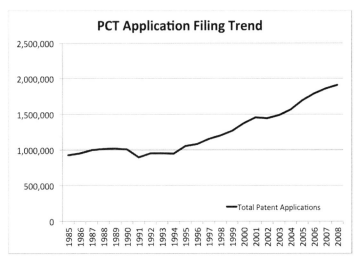

Figure Data From[12]: World Intellectual Property Indicators 2010. Authors: Economic Studies, Statistics and Analysis Division, WIPO. Publication date: September, 2010. WIPO Publication n: 941. http://www.wipo.int/ipstats/en/ statistics/patents/

Types of Work: Litigation

In patent law, litigation often deals with disputes involving patent validity, infringement, or ownership. Because litigation, by nature, involves all of the complexities of civil procedure, discovery, trial, and oral argument, it is necessary to be a qualified attorney to be fully involved in litigation. A patent agent (having passed the Patent Bar, but not having a J.D.) may, however, be involved in litigation support. A scientifically trained individual may act almost like an internal consultant by checking scientific facts, helping prepare scientific arguments, or providing an analysis of the opposition's briefs.

---

12 World Intellectual Property Organization – Economic Studies, Statistics and Analysis Division, "World Intellectual Property Indicators 2010," WIPO, http:/www.wipo.int/ipstats/en/statistics/patents/ [accessed 2010]

Litigation and patent prosecution are not usually considered compatible types of work. A patent agent may be involved in both during his early career, but as he becomes an attorney, the long-term and focused work of prosecution will not coexist easily with the intense, team based, multi-million dollar legal-hurricane of litigation. Because of this, it is a good idea to experiment with both early on. Most scientists/engineers, however, stay in prosecution because the deep study and scientific debate inherent in prosecution naturally fits their skill set. A second reason is that prosecution provides broad exposure to a variety of cutting-edge science and affords the opportunity to see the best technologies even before they are published in top journals like Science or Nature.

By contrast, the great majority of litigators in patent law are not scientists. In casual conversation I once asked a patent litigator whether he thought it would be a career advantage in litigation to have a Ph.D.

He smirked, "No. Not really."

"Why not," I asked with disbelief.

As is typical with a litigator, he was short and precise in his answer: "The Judge doesn't have a Ph.D. The jury isn't stacked with Ph.Ds. Why do I need one?"

And he was probably right. After all, if he needs scientific experts, they can be hired. Litigators don't need to be scientific experts; they need to be experts in legal research, they need to be superb speakers, persuasive writers, and be quick on their feet. By contrast, it is patent prosecution that employs many of the natural skills developed by scientists in graduate school: critical thinking, analysis, and scientific understanding. It is my opinion that most scientists are more naturally inclined to excel at prosecution.

Although it is encouraged for new patent practitioners to take part in litigation support if such opportunities arise, they will not be able to show up in the courtroom for years. Many never want to.

Types of Work: Opinion Work

A third type of work in patent law is opinion work. This encompasses all types of legal opinions that an attorney can provide to a client. A formal opinion from a lawyer is thoroughly researched and carefully considered, often over many months, and also holds significant legal weight in a court. Both of these points are important because entrepreneurs, venture capitalists, and bankers will hold a legal opinion in great esteem and use it as a decision tool to guide their business strategies, *e.g.*, to decide whether or not to invest in a new start-up company.

To more fully elaborate the importance of a legal opinion, a short illustration might me helpful: Imagine a researcher who develops an antibody to cure cancer (let's call her Dr. Jones). She is very excited and is trying to convince both venture capitalists and members of her family to invest in her new company so that she can start testing the drug in clinical trials (which are very expensive). Though her mother agrees to invest $50, the venture capitalists need more convincing. They want to be sure that no one else holds a patent that would stop Dr. Jones from making or using the drug. If someone else has patented the drug, or even the cell lines or methods used to make it, then Dr. Jones will need to license that technology or find a way to design her system around it. Obviously, the venture capitalists need to know what obstacles exist before they hand over $20 million to Dr. Jones. So, Dr. Jones calls her patent lawyer and asks him to search all of the published patents and patent applications in the United States to uncover any which might block her progress.

The opinion that her attorney produces takes 2 to 4 months of work, is about 100 pages long, and comes after an evaluation of over 1000 patents. If the attorney says that Dr. Jones's drug is "free of prior art" then the venture capitalists will be much more likely to invest. On the other hand, of someone else owns a few important patents, the attorney can act as an intermediary and make inquiries about licensing terms, analyze the patents to determine whether it is possible to argue that they are invalid, or help Dr. Jones design around the impeding technology.

But, you ask, what if the attorney makes a mistake? What if, in the course of reviewing thousands of patents, he misses or misinterprets a critical one, thereby allowing Dr. Jones to happily produce her drug and accidentally infringe on a patent? Dr. Jones may then be sued for patent infringement. But, even if she loses the case and is ordered to pay damages, her damages may be considerably reduced because she had a legal opinion from an attorney. Although that opinion missed something, it shows that Dr. Jones conducted herself in "good faith" by paying a specialist to identify possible blocking patents. In other words, she can argue that she was not a willful infringer, that this was an honest mistake, and should thus have to pay less in damages.

So, it is easy to see that a legal opinion is useful on many levels, sometimes even when that opinion is not fully correct. In the modern field of biotechology, it would be unthinkable for a pharmaceutical company or a biotech start-up to bring a new drug to market without having it thoroughly examined by a team of attorneys. The type of opinion described in Dr. Jones's case is a Freedom to Operate Opinion. It is one of the four most common types of opinions that patent attorneys provide: 1) Freedom to Operate (FTO) Opinions, 2) Invalidity Opinions, 3) Infringement Opinions, and 4) Patentability Opinions.

As described above, a FTO study involves searching patent databases and determining if there are any patents that potentially block a client's technology. This may include reviewing patents from all over the world, depending upon which countries the client intends to practice his invention or sell his product. Also, as alluded to in the example above, the search has to be broad enough in scope to capture patents on all technologies that are related to the practice of the invention. For example, if the inventor created a new doorknob, his attorney will have to search doorknobs, methods of making doorknobs, specific metal alloy compositions, locking mechanisms, etc. In a FTO study the attorney will be exclusively analyzing patent claims, not any other part of the patent. It doesn't matter to this analysis if there are other "similar" technologies out there. All that matters is whether a patent has issued with *claims* that specifically encompass the inventor's technology. As alluded to in our story, companies of all types and sizes use FTO opinions to identify potential blocking patents as they consider developing new technologies and bringing them to market. In terms of early stage investments, it is not uncommon for both the inventor and the potential investor (*e.g.*, the VC) to hire their own attorneys to prepare independent FTO analyses.

The second type of opinion, the Invalidity Opinion, is prepared in an effort to determine whether a particular patent is valid. Sometimes it is possible to conduct a thorough search of literature and find that a patented technology had already been invented before the patent was filed (meaning that the PTO didn't find the right prior art when the patent application was being examined). The most obvious way that this might be useful is when it is clear that the patent in question presents a blocking issue to an inventor or company (perhaps as discovered in an FTO analysis). If the inventor has a strong legal opinion that part or all of the patent is invalid, then he may file a countersuit to invalidate the patent or try to force its reexamination at the PTO. Alternatively, because litigation costs are so high, he may opt to license the patent anyway. In this case he can use his invalidity opinion as bargaining weight to negotiate a better licensing agreement.

The third type of opinion, the Infringement Opinion is narrower in scope and is often initiated when it is clear which patent (or set of patents) is relevant, and a client wishes to know if and how their technology infringes the patent in question. A company may also approach their attorneys to ask whether a competitor is infringing a patent. If a case for infringement can be made, the company may feel more comfortable initiating a lawsuit (or at least achieve an upper hand in licensing talks).

The fourth common opinion is the patentability opinion. In this case the analysis is centered on whether a certain invention is patentable. Another way to ask this question is, "if a patent application is filed on this invention, will any of the elements of the invention be rejected as unpatentable under 35 U.S.C. Sec. 101, 102, or 103?" In many ways this can be a broad analysis because the information in the public domain need not specifically disclose the invention to make it unpatentable. Remember that an invention must be non-obvious in view of the "art." Therefore, if public information shows that the invention would be obvious to a "skilled artisan," then the attorney would be forced to conclude that the invention is not patentable. Further note that, the "art"[13] related to a patentability study is literally anything which has been disclosed to the public anywhere on earth. As you can imagine, someone may want this type of analysis performed prior to the patenting process to determine whether the expense of filing is justified, or to get a clearer idea of what aspects of the invention are free of the art and thus should be the focus of any new applications. Oftentimes an upfront investigation like this can save a lot of money months and years down the road.

For your convenience, Table 3-1 provides an overview of the common types of legal opinions in patent law, and the types of documents examined during the preparation of each.

---

13 Be aware that "art" is a loaded term and is open to some interpretation. A document which exists in only 1 copy, and is stored in a public camping station in the Himalayas may not be prior art; however, that same single copy is definitely prior art if it is properly indexed and stored in a library.

Table 3-1

Research in Legal Opinions		
Opinion	**Types of Documents Analyzed**	**Relevant Jurisdictions**
Freedom to Operate	Patents only, focusing on claims.	Any countries in which the client intends to practice, produce, or sell the invention.
Invalidity	Any documents, media, or products in use. Pay attention to the published prosecution history of the patent in question. Documents include patents, journal articles, newspapers, advertisements, etc. It is possible to invalidate some claims of a patent without invalidating the entire claim set.	All countries.
Infringement	The analysis will likely surround the specific patent or patent family in question (e.g., the client may ask, "Do we infringe patent X?") The focus of the analysis will be on the claims, i.e., do the claims cover your client's invention?	Infringement determinations are specific to the any particular jurisdiction of interest.
Patentability	Any document, media, or product in use.	All countries.

Due Diligence

The term "due diligence" can mean a number of things depending upon the industry in which you work. In the realm of technology companies and venture capital firms due diligence is, broadly, the detailed inspection of a company prior to a merger, acquisition, investment, or contract agreement. This inspection may cover all aspects of the firm including its management, finances, business plan, and assets. For a technology company, one of the most critical assets is intellectual property. Therefore, to a patent specialist, due diligence will focus on the analysis of a company's intellectual property position.

Despite the narrowing of our definition, due diligence is still an amorphous subject because it may encompass a number of different types of analyses depending on the stage of technology development, and the reasons for the investigation. In the context of a merger or acquisition, the analysis may be so broad as to encompass a company's entire patent estate. But, if someone is interested in licensing a specific technology, the diligence may be focused only on a certain patent or portfolio.

As one example, consider a large pharmaceutical company deciding whether to license or buy the rights to a small patent estate. The due diligence in this case will be related to patents only. The pharmaceutical company will want to be sure that the patents are strong (*i.e.*, they cannot be easily invalidated) and they will want to be certain that the patents completely cover the technology they wish to employ.

On the other extreme is due diligence with respect to a venture capital investment[14]. In such situations a startup is in negotiations to acquire financing from a venture capital firm. Both the startup and the VCs will generally hire their own IP counsel. VC investment negotiations can be very adversarial, and the IP counsel for the VC will thoroughly examine the patent applications and the technology of the firm,

---

14 Please do not confuse this discussion with the broader due diligence conducted by the VCs prior to investment. The discussion here is relevant only to intellectual property. Aside from IP, VCs will examine all aspects of a business, from balance sheets to employee reputations.

trying to find any flaw that might influence their investment decision or negotiating position. The VC will clearly not invest without the approval of their legal counsel. The efforts of the patent lawyer on behalf of the VC firm are at least two fold. First, if IP attorney finds that the patents are invalid or that they will not adequately cover the company's technology, then they can save the VC from a bad investment. Second, if the attorney finds that the company's patents are valid but potentially weak, then the VC may use this information to his benefit during negotiations. If the patent portfolio is a risky bet the VC may have reason to demand a larger stake in the company.

4

CHAPTER FOUR

Career Progression

The purpose of this chapter is to illuminate the career path that is generally followed by a scientist in intellectual property law. In my experience, it is not easy to find information on intellectual property careers that is tailored to science professionals newly entering the field. There is plenty of information for law school students (such as what to study for the patent bar or what kind of coursework qualifies you to take the patent bar.). What is usually missing for the scientist is information on how law school tuition is paid, whether there are obligations to a law firm in return for tuition money, how many billable hours are usually required while attending law school, etc.

In order to approach these subjects in a self-contained way, I want to first describe the basic career progression and types of law firms. I have organized the remainder of the chapter as a set of frequently asked questions, followed by detailed answers. One question that often arises is "What is your work like?" or "What is a typical day like?" Because this is such a frequent (and important) question, I have dedicated part of chapter 6 to describing a typical day for patent practitioners at various levels of a law firm.

Basic Career Timeline

Figure 4-1 depicts a general timeline for a career path ranging from entry into patent law through partnership at a law firm. As discussed in previous chapters, a science professional will usually enter the field of patent law after a Ph.D. or M.D. (in life sciences) or possibly a M.S. degree if she is an engineer or computer scientist. The entry level position is called a technical specialist[15] or "tech-spec" for short. Most law firms will prefer that at tech-spec work at the firm for a full year before beginning law school. Once law school begins, the tech-spec works at his firm during the day and attends law school in the evening. This difficult schedule is usually compensated for by a reduction in required hours in the office.

Don't think that the reduction of working hours in any way constitutes a conversion to "part time" work. Your responsibilities at the law firm will remain largely unchanged. Last minute filings and unexpected disclosures from clients may still press your working schedule into the evenings or weekends, sometimes forcing you to miss class. Even if your firm is attentive to your needs and completely respectful of your class time (and not all firms are) you will find that the work/class combination is an extraordinary challenge. The problem is not that any of your work to too difficult to do, but just that there is so much on your plate that the responsibilities feel incessant. When work is finished, class is over, reading is done, and your legal writing assignments are complete, you will find that there is little energy or time left for anything but rest. Time management is key, as well as knowing when to give yourself a break.

Evening law school programs take about four years to complete. Before the completion of law school, most tech-specs choose to study for and take the Patent Bar exam. Law firms may differ on when they prefer you to pass the Patent Bar. Some firms put more emphasis on training within the firm and will allow their employees to take the exam whenever they feel comfortable, perhaps even after law school graduation. By

---

15 Technical specialist is the most common term although some firms use "technology specialist," "science advisor," or some similar variation.

contrast, other firms want their patent professionals registered to practice as early as possible so that they can take on more responsibility for their work (*i.e.,* they can actually file the patents they write with the PTO rather than relying on an attorney or partner to sign the paperwork).

Finally, upon the completion of law school and passage of the state bar exam, the tech-spec (or Patent Agent if he has passed the Patent Bar) will become a full associate. Usually a fresh J.D. graduate is called a first year associate; however, because a tech-spec has worked in law for at least 4 or 5 years by the time they attain the J.D., they are often given credit for their advanced tenure. The credit received may differ from firm to firm, but it is safe to say that a fresh tech-spec J.D. can expect to be at least a 3rd year associate after passing the state bar exam. From that point, progression to senior associate and partner can take anywhere from 4 to 12 years depending upon firm policy, performance, politics, and a host of other factors.

As you consider these timelines, please keep in mind that they are only one possibility among many. Everyone's experience will be different. Some people, for one reason or another, take leave from law school and require 5 or 6 years to complete the J.D. Some may decide to pay for law school by themselves instead of going the tech-spec route. Others may know very early that they love patent law and pass the patent bar even before they finish their scientific degrees. Still others may express their interest in patents differently and become a patent Examiner before going to law school (or perhaps choose patent examination as their final career). The point is that there is no single defined career path, and you will have to choose the route that is right for you.

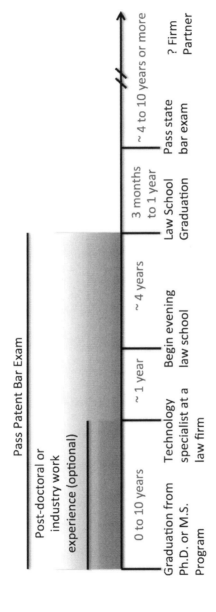

Pass Patent Bar Exam

Post-doctoral or industry work experience (optional)

0 to 10 years	~ 1 year	~ 4 years	3 months to 1 year	~ 4 to 10 years or more
Graduation from Ph.D. or M.S. Program	Technology specialist at a law firm	Begin evening law school	Law School Graduation	Pass state bar exam
				? Firm Partner

Timeline depicting a typical path from technology expert, through initial training at a law firm, and eventually on to full attorney and firm partner. Although many people enter patent law after post-doctoral or industry work experience, there are also many who do not. The timeline indicates that passing the patent bar is a flexible requirement that may be met at a range of times beginning prior to law firm entry or even after attainment of the J.D. degree.

As you begin tailoring your resume to apply to law firms, you will notice that firms differ drastically in their size and expertise. Do you want to be at a huge, powerful firm that engages in high stakes litigation? Would you prefer a very prestigious global firm, even if it has a relatively small patent practice; or, do you feel that you would gain deeper expertise at a smaller firm that focuses exclusively on patent prosecution?

Unless you are lucky, you won't really have to make this decision early in your career because you may only have one or two initial job offers. Nevertheless, whether you wish to work for a large, general practice firm, or a small intellectual property boutique will determine how you move forward in your career.

General practice firms will usually have more resources and better name recognition. Some of these firms (*e.g.*, Skadden or Baker and McKenzie) are global and have over a billion dollars of revenue every year. Another quality of Big Law is that they have traditionally dealt much more heavily in patent litigation than in prosecution, chiefly because big litigation requires significant upfront resources and because it is a high reward business. This laser focus on IP litigation in big firms has been changing in recent years as national and global law firms expand their ranks of patent prosecutors or simply buy up smaller IP boutiques.

When considering a career move into a large firm, it is important to get an understanding of how they manage patent prosecution. Don't be afraid to ask probing questions in your interview. IP prosecution requires a unique set of resources and infrastructure. These include specialized dockets and docket managers, staff to prepare and file international patents, specially trained patent assistants, and expert patent paralegals, just to name a few. Such supportive infrastructure may be partly absent or poorly managed at some firms, especially if they have only a small prosecution practice. This oversight is not necessarily intentional neglect, but may arise because firm decision makers either don't appreciate the unique aspects of IP prosecution or are too busy with other practice areas to invest considerable resources in what amounts to a small part of the firm. Remember that patent prosecution does not have the same high profit margins as litigation does. A larger firm may choose (perhaps wisely) to focus their resources in other areas. Maintaining a patent prosecution group helps the firm grow patent expertise and helps when cross-selling services from the litigation department.

The facts above should not discourage you from considering Big Law. Indeed, some large firms highly value their prosecution practices and sustain more patent attorneys than do specialized boutiques. If you take the plunge into Big Law, you may find it rewarding to be exposed to a variety of law practice areas. For example, your patent work may lead you to support litigation teams, venture capital due diligence teams, or corporate lawyers as they negotiate mergers and acquisitions. The deep interconnections between IP, mergers, acquisitions, negotiations, and investments has recently been referred to as "corporate IP," and there has been much discussion about this becoming the new frontier of intellectual property in big business[16].

On the other hand, many attorneys and industry leaders feel that the greatest concentration of IP expertise and scientific knowledge exists in IP boutique firms. The IP boutique usually consists of anywhere between 5 and 50 patent attorneys, although some boutiques have grown national in scope (*e.g.*, Finnegan Henderson employs over 370 attorneys focused on IP). Essentially all attorneys in the boutique will be focused on IP, allowing these seemingly small firms to retain more experts in patents than many of their Big Law counterparts. The deep pool of experience at boutiques offers an unparalleled training ground for a newcomer to the field. Furthermore, because they have so many attorneys and agents with Ph.D.'s in a variety of fields, boutiques offer scientific expertise that is often not seen outside of university science departments or corporate research centers. The collegial atmosphere and academic pedigree present in most boutiques can make for an easier transition for scientists beginning their careers in law.

---

16   Bringardner, J. "The New Breed of IP Lawyer: A Combination of Corporate Law Smarts and IP Expertise", IP Law & Business, April 19, 2007; http://www.law.com/jsp/article.jsp?id=900005554710

When should I apply to a law firm?
Should I go to law school first or maybe pass the patent bar before I apply?

As discussed above, you can apply to a firm directly after completing a Masters (maybe) or Ph.D. degree. It is equally common for applicants to have completed post-doctoral work or a few years in industry before applying. There are no hard and fast rules: you should begin your applications as soon as you know that you wish to enter the field. I have seen many scientists enter law firms as late as age 35 or 40, and I'm sure others have started later than that. At first impression you may feel that such candidates will be at a disadvantage (with respect to career advancement) to younger Ph.D. graduates because they have come so late to the field. To the contrary, more experienced candidates are generally more confident in themselves and their new career choice. They are likely to have had leadership experience and are thus better equipped to handle clients and quickly take on responsibility. More often than not, this is a recipe for success. Don't be afraid to make the switch because you think it's too late.

Most new applicants fast become aware that patent law is a hard field to break into. If you find yourself past your second round of applications with no luck, then consider taking the Patent Bar. Becoming a patent agent demonstrates to potential employers that you are serious about entering the field, and they will also be confident that, because you already know the basics, you will need less initial training.

What is a billable hour? How many billable hours are (usually) required in patent law?

Put simply, a billable hour is an hour of work for which you can bill a client. This will constitute only the time you spend specifically working on a client's project, not counting time you spend on lunch, coffee, and other tasks that are part of a normal workday.

Billable hours are an efficient mechanism of capturing how much time you actually spend on each task and project. It is also a controversial topic because many associates dislike being required to bill a set number of hours and many clients dislike the uncertainty associated with a system that doesn't provide them with flat rate fees that can be easily budgeted. Nevertheless, patent work is complex, and no two projects are the same. Law firms will argue that the billable hour system is the fairest way to capture and bill for the varying difficulty of different projects.

Billing an 8-hour day usually means spending 9 or 9.5 hours in the office if you work efficiently. Big Law firms traditionally require between 1800 and 2200 hours per year, though these requirements are trending lower in patent practices in order to stay competitive with boutique firms that require no more than 1850 to 1900 hours at a maximum. When taking evening courses at law school, almost all firms will lower the billable hour requirement to 1500 or 1600 hours.

What should I study to pass the patent bar?

Theoretically, everything you need to pass the patent bar is in the Manual for Patent Examining procedure (MPEP), which may be found online at:

http://www.uspto.gov/web/offices/pac/mpep/mpep.htm

The MPEP will also be available in electronic form while you take the exam. Yes, the exam is open book. Unfortunately, because the exam covers so much material, it is very important to memorize and internalize a great deal of material before taking the test. Because of this, the test is doubtlessly easier for someone with a year or two of practice under their belt.

The exam itself consists of 100 multiple-choice questions broken into two 3-hour sessions; however, only 90 of the 100 questions are graded. The additional 10 questions are considered "experimental."[17] A passing score for the patent bar is 70%, meaning that you only need

---

17 Quinn, G., IPWatchdog, http://www.ipwatchdog.com/patent-bar-exam/ [accessed April 25, 2009];

to answer 63 questions correctly [please note that the test and format may change periodically and you should check the PTO website for the most up to date information]. Despite this, the exam is a difficult one and has had a pass rate as low as 50% in the past.[17] Many test takers choose to enroll in a professional Patent Bar Review course prior to signing up for the test. The course will provide several days of intense instruction, and most will also provide a copy of the MPEP, a concise set of notes and examples, and software that simulates the actual exam.

In my own personal experience, the two most common professional review courses are offered by PRG (Patent Resources Group) and PLI (the Practicing Law Institute). Both have an excellent reputation. I took the course offered by PRG and found it extremely helpful. The notes and materials were thoughtful and well prepared, and the instructors were incredibly knowledgeable. Many of the speakers were practicing attorneys who filled the lectures with interesting anecdotes about situations they have seen in their law firms. Arguably the most useful study tool is the simulated exam software, which allows you to take randomized exams based on previous bar exam questions. The software times your test, grades it for you, and also provides model answers and links to the relevant material in the MPEP. The linking to the MPEP is invaluable in helping you get comfortable navigating the manual, a necessary exam skill.

Whatever you do, don't underestimate the complexity of the exam or think it will be easy because it is open book. It is not always clear where to look for an answer, and, if you try to look up too many questions, you probably won't finish the test in time. I felt that I was efficient at looking up topics in the index and finding the answers in the MPEP. I still only just finished the exam in the time allotted.

How many years will law school take? Will I only be a first year associate after I graduate?

In the typical path, a scientist enters the law firm as a technical specialist and works there for approximately 1 year before law school begins. This arrangement allows a newcomer to get familiar with work at a law firm before being thrust into the rigors of first year law school.

Law school itself takes 4 years of evening classes to complete. Although some firms will allow their technical specialists to take day classes (and work part-time, evenings and weekends) this is an extreme rarity. The only way to arrive at the J.D. faster than four years is to take summer courses if possible. Two full summers of courses may allow you to graduate one semester early (*i.e.*, you will finish in 3.5 years instead of 4). Some students, for personal or other reasons, may also take a temporary leave from law school, thereby drawing out their graduation to 5 or even 6 years.

One of the major perks of taking the tech-spec path (besides the fact that the firm pays for your education) is that you will often be given some credit for your years of experience once you have the J.D. Rather than becoming a first year associate when you graduate, you may directly become a third or fourth year associate. Every firm will have a different policy on this, so you should speak to the hiring committee about their policy when you join the firm.

How long does it take to make partner?

In general, a 7th or 8th year associate will be seriously thinking about when he or she will make partner. For someone starting out as a technical specialist, the whole process, from law school to associate, to partner may take 9 to 12 years, although this can vary considerably. In some places partnership has more than one level. For example, some firms offer "non-equity" partnerships whereby the attorney may consider themselves partner because they have management responsibility (and get paid more than an associate), yet not actually be part-owner of the firm.

In some unusual cases, someone with great experience and excellent performance can make partner when they are a 4th or 5th year associate.

What is the typical starting salary for a technology specialist, a patent agent, and a patent attorney?

An average starting salary for an inexperienced technology specialist (*i.e.*, a fresh Ph.D. with no knowledge of patent law) can fall anywhere from $50,000/year to $115,000/year, depending on the market, the economy, and the law firm. In my personal experience, I have seen entry-level technology specialists receive starting salaries of between $80k and $100k in the Boston area (a very robust patent market) just prior to the 2008 financial crisis. As usual, large general practice firms may pay more but also have a higher billable hour requirement. This salary range will be similar for a patent agent with no law firm experience. A first year patent attorney (J.D.) may expect a salary in the range of $100,000 to $160,000 with the higher amounts being paid in general practice firms in large markets like New York City or San Francisco. Because of the recent financial crisis of 2008 and 2009, many associates have had their salaries frozen, and starting salaries have been falling somewhat. Many believe that patent law is partly insulated from this salary reduction mainly because patent professionals are so highly qualified and because patent work often tends to remain robust, at least during the early parts of a recession. Also, during times of financial hardship, companies may be more vigorous about defending their intellectual property rights. Nevertheless, turning down a salary of even $70,000 would be foolish in today's market. If you are interested in exploring recent data for starting salaries, the discussion boards at www.intelproplaw.com can be very useful as well as the links posted in the footnote at the bottom of this page.[18] At least until the recent financial crisis, the salary progression in law has been steep. Yearly salary increases can run from 5-10% of base salary in good years, and bonuses can reach $20-$30,000 in some firms for full attorneys.

---

18   For more up to date salary information, check the following: http://www.glassdoor.com/Salaries/patent-technical-specialist-salary-SRCH_KO0,27.htm, http://www.simplyhired.com/a/salary/search/q-patent+technical+specialist

Once I become a lawyer, what other career options will be available?

Although it is difficult to think about what you may want to do 4 or 5 years from now, there are a number of options open to you once you have a J.D. Remember that, whatever your prior experience, you will become a fully qualified lawyer. There will be nothing stopping you from practicing estate law, family law, or corporate law if you truly prefer those areas of work. Literally anything from politics to policy positions will be potentially open to you. Such a change may not be easy, though, since all of your experience will be in patents and science. It would be a bad idea to enter patent law with the idea that you will leave it in 5 or 6 years for another discipline. The reason is that it requires passion and commitment to be successful at patent law, especially when attending law school and working full time. If you view patent law as merely a stepping-stone to something else, you may be setting yourself up for several unhappy and unsatisfying years.

Will I have a chance to do both patent prosecution and litigation?

Probably not right away. As a scientific specialist is it very possible that you will be brought into litigation projects as an expert to analyze patents and help in the preparation of arguments. However, many of the big firms specifically separate the litigation groups from the patent prosecution groups, and boutique firms usually aren't as active in litigation.

Aside from basic scientific analysis, there is good reason why more junior people don't work on litigation immediately. One is that the work is intense and may require very long hours. More importantly, preparing the legal arguments, briefs, and memos necessary for litigation requires specialist skills in legal writing and civil procedure that can only be gained by experience, first in law school but primarily after the J.D.

What is law school like? How do I balance work and school?

Law school requires entirely different study habits than most science and engineering courses. However, despite all the hype that law school is terribly difficult (think of the movie, Paperchase), it isn't overwhelming by itself. The challenge of law school for a technical specialist is not the classwork alone, but the combination of full time work and evening courses. Law firm life is unpredictable, wrought with last minute client requests and unexpected evening and weekend casework. This means that missing classes is an all too frequent event, and you can't always count on weekend time to catch up with studying.

The first year of law school is the most structured. Most required courses are completed in the first year, with the later two years left for specialization and electives. In an evening program, the required courses will be spread out over the first two years. A typical first year evening semester includes Contract law, Civil Procedure, Criminal Law, and Legal Practice Skills (sometimes called legal writing). These courses will continue in the second semester, with the exception of Criminal Law, which may be replaced with the Law of Torts. Further required courses include Constitutional Law and Property Law, which may be taken in the second year of the evening program.[19] Many students choose to tailor their schedule to the subjects that will appear on their specific state bar exam. For this reason, Evidence and a state specific civil practice course are often recommended. A course in professional responsibility and ethics is also usually required.

Most law school courses operate on the Socratic system. Legal principles are taught in the context of previously decided court cases. As the student, your job is to read the court opinions and be prepared to discuss the legal principles in class. Professors call on students

---

19 The schedule I describe here is based on my experience at Suffolk University Law School, which has a well respected evening program. The required courses are largely uniform between law schools (as prescribed by the ABA), but your particular experience may vary slightly.

randomly, and it could hurt your grade if you are unprepared to discuss a case, or are absent when called. Depending upon the professor, you will be questioned about the various aspects of the case, until you begin to falter in your answers. Besides the independent preparation for class discussion, there is little other assigned work. Although this system sounds scary, in practical terms you may not be called upon to speak at all. Considering that there are only so many classes per semester, if a class has 80 to 100 students, you may slip by completely unnoticed. But, to get the top grades it is certainly necessary to speak up. While some professors will not dock points for silence, they may give bonus points for class contributions.

Most first year law school courses are graded almost entirely on a final exam, and sometimes partly on a mid-term exam. Keeping up with law school reading is complicated further by the fact that most first year law school students need to take a course in legal practice skills ("LPS," or legal writing in some schools). This course teaches legal research and writing and so does not operate on the case-based Socratic system. In LPS there are regular writing and research assignments due almost weekly. Completing these assignments can further erode precious weekends and detract from time that could otherwise be used to prepare for the more theoretical classes. In my opinion, LPS is the reason that first year law school is usually considered to be the most difficult year.

The amount of "required" reading in school is truly enormous. To read every case and prepare case briefs[20], as professors suggest, is next to impossible while working. Those students who wish to be in the top 2%-5% of the class *must* put in that effort. Traditionally, law school students struggle to get into the top 10% of the class in order to be taken seriously as a potential associate at a big law firm. The situation is slightly different for a technical specialist, however, because he or she is already employed and gaining experience.

Most of the professionals in the field with whom I have spoken generally agree that grades are less important for a scientist/tech-spec. Keep in mind that all classes are graded on a curve. In general, the top

---

20 A case brief is a short case synopsis that summarizes the facts, the court's decision, the rule of law that the court relied upon, and the court's reasoning.

5 or 10% of the class will get an A, another 10-15% will get a B+ to A-, 36-44% will get a B- or B, 30-40% will get a C or C+, and the remainder, usually 10% or less, will get a C- or lower (which is considered failing)[21]. So, it is clearly difficult to get a top grade because you need to be within the best 5-10% of the class. By the same calculus, it is equally difficult to fail. This means that studying in law school is an exercise in diminishing returns. A reasonable amount of studying will achieve a passing, albeit average, grade. A bit more effort and you can get a B or B+. Beyond that, it is necessary to commit more and more time to achieve moderate improvements in grade. For those who need to establish an excellent track record in order to land that Big Law job in Manhattan, the extra effort is essential (law professor jobs in academia also tend to require excellent grades). For others already working in patent law, grades may be less important on balance, although you should always remember that poor grades can have a negative impact on your career. Some law firms even insist on a minimum performance or they will not pay for the class credits.

One important aspect of law school that may come as a surprise to those trained in the sciences is the emphasis on class outlining. Course outlining is a staple of law school life with students getting into study groups near the end of the semester to "outline" the course. For those looking to save some energy the school bookstores sell general outlines for all the basic first year courses, and old student outlines can be found all over the internet. A good course outline contains the principles of law taught in the course and a list of the relevant cases including the facts, rules of law, and case holdings. Upon entering law school, the concept of creating your own outline seems redundant, especially when commercial casebooks and outlines are available. Nevertheless, writing out your own outline is an effective form of studying in itself, and there is no replacement for having a single source of material from which to study. My recommendation is to use your daily class notes in combination with commercial case briefs and outlines to prepare your

---

21   This example was taken from the suggested curve of Suffolk University in 2009, though other schools will be similar: http://www.law.suffolk.edu/offices/deanofstu/handbook/regs/rule3.cfm

own customized study outlines. One great source of free study aids is the Lexis Nexis Area of Law Outlines available at:

http://www.lexisnexis.com/lawschool/study/outlines/default.asp.

You can download these outlines in MS Word format and add to them or rearrange them as you see fit.

There are no easy answers on how to balance work and school. It is very important to learn how to prioritize and balance expectations. If you are like most people, you will have three competing priorities: work, family, and school. Since you are in the office for a set number of hours and you have a duty to clients, your work will often have to be a first priority. In many situations school will have to take a back seat to family and work. Although you undoubtedly have an internal drive to achieve the best possible grades, you must learn to accept that you can't do everything perfectly. If you have a type-A personality and expect yourself to be the top performer at everything you do, you may end up feeling as if you are failing a little bit at every task. It is all right to compromise sometimes. The bottom line is that, unless you are superhuman, you can't get a 4.0 average, be a star at work, and be the perfect wife, sister, or mom. Don't be afraid to take a weekend off to escape and recharge. If you don't, you run the danger of burning out.

Other considerations on adjusting to life in law

One important thing I felt unprepared for when entering law was a change in my self-perception. I had spent years thinking of myself as a scientist, perhaps a future professor. In academia it is easy to fall into the trap of thinking that a research career is the only noble or worthwhile career in the world. After all, isn't it research on new technologies that drives business?.... isn't it research that motivates intellectual property?....research that makes medicine, construction, and engineering more useful to all of us??? And of course, what is more noble than unraveling the mysteries of nature? Surely that is more important than preparing legal memos and shoveling through piles of bureaucracy every day! Right??

This kind of bias in academia is widespread and difficult to surmount. One scientist I know discussed the merits of academia and said something along these lines-- "Anyone who can get a Ph.D. could earn a million dollars in business. But, you should spend your time doing something more important and more meaningful with your life."

Thus, being a "scientist" became part of my identity. The question facing me was "how do I come to think of myself as a 'lawyer' after spending the last 10 years studying biochemistry and mathematics?" The truth is that there are deep scholarly foundations to the law, based on principles of philosophy, science, business, ethics, and social responsibility. As you read cases in law school, you come to appreciate the deep thinking and profound intellect that goes into judicial opinions and legal arguments. Although the law may feel arbitrary sometimes, there are often sophisticated reasons that it develops along certain lines, and (despite overpublicized abuses) you quickly gain the sense that there are brilliant and thoughtful people working hard to get the decisions right...people who believe that law is necessary to create a just and stable society. Similarly, you begin to appreciate how all of business, science, and society sits within a protective legal framework. Without contract and securities law, business would be chaotic. Without criminal law, society would be barbaric. Without regulatory law, drugs and foods would be unsafe and untested. And, without patent law innovation would stagnate. A lawyer, you will learn, is a guardian and a guide who protects the basic rights of their clients and helps them navigate a system that is too complex for many laymen. Indeed, the success of a business (and its technologies) relies not only on the science, but also equally on the contracts, licenses, and patents which form its basic foundations.

It is clear that people will have a variety of opinions on the value of law in society. But my point in all this is that the scholarly work of science and the scholarly work of law are not that different conceptually. At the very least, they are equal pillars in a stable, progressing society. Still, even with a full appreciation for law in the world, you will be left with the original questions: Is a lawyer what you truly want to be or are you a scientist? If the search for new knowledge and the study of nature is part of who you are... if you feel that being a "scientist" is too much a part of you, then you may have difficulty, as many people do, in reworking your self-image as lawyer. Such a steep career change can require more self-reflection than is immediately apparent.

Law is ok, but I really just want to make more money. Will I be happy at a law firm?

Absolutely not! Surely, a job at a law firm pays more than many other careers. But, I have seen that the people who are truly successful have a passion for the practice of law. I say "the practice of law" because studying law and practicing it are two entirely different things, just as studying biology and working in a laboratory are very different. It is quite possible to thoroughly enjoy law school, love analyzing cases, and yet completely dislike practicing law.

Law school professors and scholars spend their time examining issues, studying public policy, and writing research articles. Thus, they spend a great deal of their time thinking and weighing theories against reality. In law school you may prepare legal memos and briefs, but you will often have many weeks to do so, giving you the time to refine and revise your arguments to perfection.

By contrast, a young lawyer in a law practice must turn out an argument or a memo in a few hours. A lawyer is a service provider. Efficiency is prized. There is little time to weigh policy ideas or the merits of a judicial decision. Instead, the goal is simply to understand the tenets of the law and represent your client as best as possible, in as little time as is reasonable to do the job well. This requires the ability to produce many documents and arguments quickly. Those who are successful in law firms enjoy (or at least don't mind) working on deadlines everyday. They also take pleasure in in the challenge of managing a full and complex calendar, and it doesn't bother them that most of their professional and social lives will be built around that calendar. Law practice also requires a lot more administrative work than many people would like. While writing a patent is an intellectually challenging task, many of the other elements of prosecution (*e.g.,* preparing sequence listings, information disclosure statements, and power of attorney documents) are not particularly engaging but nonetheless time consuming.

Also, truly successful lawyers have a great attention to detail. "Attention to detail" has become somewhat of a catchall phase in the business world, but it really has a deeper substance in the practice of law. Did you use the word *"invention"* or *"claimed invention,"* in that patent application, because it can make a difference? Did you double-check those DNA sequences (one missing letter can completely change that drug you are claiming)? Did you thoroughly look through those 5000 patent abstracts? Were any of the abstracts relevant to your client's technology? You quickly realize that, in law, "attention to detail" really means "tireless, unwavering, meticulous attention to detail."

On top of all this, lawyers are widely reported to be some of the unhappiest workers in the professional world[22,23]. My favorite blog post on this topic, which may be more entertaining than informative, can be found at: http://blogs.wsj.com/law/2007/07/16/british-lawyers-are-unhappy-too/. [24]

My point in all of this is not to claim that practicing law is a boring, administrative burden. Rather, I want to highlight that you should have a true interest and passion for the law and for providing service to clients before you decide that you want to spend your life at a law firm. Every career has its merits and drawbacks. While law has innumerable merits, it still takes a genuine passion to excel when the work is interesting and still be effective when it is not. Someone with passion will perceive the administrative details as merely additional opportunities to represent their clients. However, if you take the job for money alone, every day in the office will begin to feel like a stream of never ending law school assignments: endless deadlines with real responsibility attached. *Bottom-line:* Don't go into legal practice unless you feel that you have (or have a strong potential for developing) a real and true love for the

---

22 Ward, S.F., "Pulse of the Legal Profession," ABA Journal. October 2007 Issue, http://www.abajournal.com/magazine/article/pulse_of_the_legal_profession/ [accessed August 4th, 2011]

23 Sanghera, S., "Why are Lawyers Miserable? Want a list?, " The Times, July 9th, 2007, http://business.timesonline.co.uk/tol/business/law/article2045254.ece [accessed August 4, 2011].

24 Peter Lattman, "British Lawyers are Unhappy, Too," The Wall Street Journal Law Blog, entry posted July 16th 2007, http://blogs.wsj.com/law/2007/07/16/british-lawyers-are-unhappy-too/ [accessed August 4th 2011].

practice of law and for representing clients. Money or a need to escape the laboratory bench are not good reasons.

What if I have a bachelor's degree (in science or engineering) but I have not been to graduate school? Can I still compete in the field?

If you have only a bachelor's degree it is still possible to be a fully qualified and successful patent practitioner. Remember that the idea of a technical specialist (*i.e.*, someone with a Ph.D. who attends law school at night while working full time at a firm) has only been around for about 20 years now. Many of the most senior intellectual property attorneys are not doctors and I will guess that most do not have graduate degrees other than a J.D. Lack of a Ph.D. or Master's degree will certainly not bar you from entering the field. That said, you should make sure that your classes in science qualify you to take the Patent Bar exam, for which you must have a technical or scientific degree. If not, you may need to take a few courses to meet the requirements. Also, without a Ph.D. it is much less likely that a law firm will hire you before you acquire a J.D. In general, a Ph.D. is a more valued degree in the life sciences that it is in the engineering disciplines. Accordingly, it is not uncommon to see computer or electrical engineers being hired as technical specialists with only a B.S. or M.S. degree (though increasing numbers do have Ph.D.'s). In the life sciences, a Ph.D. is becoming a prerequisite for a technical specialist job. Without it, you will have to consider putting yourself through law school and completing the patent bar before you can expect to work at a law firm. But please remember that the needs and expectations of every firm may be different. It is always best to talk to local attorneys, partners, and recruiters to figure out what accomplishments are most sought after in your local market.

If you do decide that putting yourself through law school is the right choice for you, don't think of it as too much of a disadvantage. Working in the day and attending class at night is a very difficult schedule to maintain for four years. Even if you have to take on debt to get through law school, you will at least have the chance to give your full attention to class, thereby allowing you to enjoy a more balanced life while you're studying. Look on the bright side. While you may take some loans for a three year J.D., you will bypass the 5-7 year Ph.D. and the subsequent four-year evening law program. Although it may be true that you cannot compete with a Ph.D. for a technical specialist job, if you do well in law school you should be able to compete effectively once you have the J.D. and pass the patent bar. Just make sure you think carefully about the educational debt you plan to take on, and make sure that it is something you can afford in the long term even if you don't land your dream job at a patent law firm.

5

CHAPTER FIVE

Getting the Job: Your Resume and Cover Letter

Before we tackle some of the more interesting aspects of job-hunting in patent law, it is important to say a few words about the basics. No matter how qualified or connected you are, no matter who you know or how good you are at patent law, you will never land that first job if your resume and cover letter are sub-standard. This section contains a few examples of actual resumes and cover letters, as well as some points to remember when preparing them. Let's start with three similar example resumes:

Resume - Format 1

JOHN SMITH, Ph.D.
42 Cranberry Lane
Anytown MA, 12345
(123) 456-7891 - jsmith@email.com

EDUCATION

IVY UNIVERSITY, Ph.D. Molecular Biology;	**GPA: 3.82**	**May, 2009**

Honors: To University President's Fellowship
Teaching Fellow for Genetics Lab
Research: Designed statistical models of human and gene regulation. Tested 4 lead compounds to target malignant glioma. Named inventor on 2 U.S. Patent Applications
Presented research at 4 departmental seminars and 3 conferences in Canada and Austria.

STATE UNIVERSITY, B.S Biology;	**GPA: 3.63**	**May, 2004**

Honors: Full Scholarship from Biology Department
Award for undergraduate research poster: 2003
Genetics department stipend for summer research
Research: Prepared a thesis for a project designed to generate mutant yeast strains that produce novel anti-cancer antibodies.
Further research included performing experiments including northern blots, fluorescence microscopy, NMR, PCR, and microbiological isolation.

EXPERIENCE

CONSULTANT START-UP BIOTECHNOLOGIES   2011 – Spring
- Advised on and implemented a system to screen gene expression data for drug candidates to treat non-Hodgkin's lymphoma.
- Worked closely with the company founders to train scientists on the analysis system.

SCIENTIST, CANCER RESEARCH COMPANY   2009 – Present
- Analysis of genomic data produced by next generation sequencing platforms including full human and cancer genomic sequences.
- Analyzed DNA and RNA from 10 skin cancer patients in an effort to identify polymorphisms that correlate with invasive cancer.

INTERN, IVY UNIVERSITY TECHNOLOGY TRANSFER OFFICE   2007 – 2009
- Contributed research reports and summaries during venture capital due diligence. Presented marketability recommendations on several technologies to the chief of business development.
- Organized patent filing system and assisted with the evaluation of technology disclosures.

TEACHING FELLOW, IVY UNIVERSITY   2006
- Organized and led laboratory discussions and field experiments for a class of 40 students.
- Prepared and graded genetics laboratory exams. Participated in Teaching Organization and Leadership seminars

PUBLICATIONS
- **Smith J**, Kevins M, DeLoite C (2008) Treatment Regimes for Glioma. *Biology Journal*, 3:22.
- **Smith J**,. DeLoite C (2005) A review of Gene Expression Analysis for Cancer. *Important Reviews*, 5:21.
- Jenkins, R, **Smith J**, Kevins M (2007) A New Gene Expression Analysis System. *Biology Journal*, 7:18.

58

Resume Format 2

JOHN SMITH, Ph.D.
42 Cranberry Lane
Anytown MA, 12345
(123)456-7891 - jsmith@email.com

EDUCATION

IVY UNIVERSITY, Ph.D. Molecular Biology;   **GPA: 3.82**   **May, 2009**

Honors: To University President's Fellowship
Teaching Fellow for Genetics Lab

Research: Designed statistical models of human and gene regulation. Tested 4 lead compounds to target malignant glioma. Named inventor on 2 U.S. Patent Applications
Presented research at 4 departmental seminars and 3 conferences in Canada and Austria.

STATE UNIVERSITY, B.S Biology;   **GPA: 3.63**   **May, 2004**

Honors: Full Scholarship from Biology Department
Award for undergraduate research poster: 2003
Genetics department stipend for summer research

Research: Prepared a thesis for a project designed to generate mutant yeast strains that produce novel anti-cancer antibodies.
Further research included performing experiments including northern blots, fluorescence microscopy, NMR, PCR, and microbiological isolation.

EXPERIENCE

CONSULTANT START-UP BIOTECHNOLOGIES   **2011 – Spring**
Advised on and implemented a system to screen gene expression data for drug candidates to treat non-Hodgkin's lymphoma. Worked closely with the company founders to train scientists on the analysis system.

SCIENTIST, CANCER RESEARCH COMPANY   **2009 – Present**
Analysis of genomic data produced by next generation sequencing platforms including full human and cancer genomic sequences.
Analyzed DNA and RNA from 10 skin cancer patients in an effort to identify polymorphisms that correlate with invasive cancer.

INTERN, IVY UNIVERSITY TECHNOLOGY TRANSFER OFFICE   **2007 – 2009**
Contributed research reports and summaries during venture capital due diligence. Presented marketability recommendations on several technologies to the chief of business development.
Organized patent filing system and assisted with the evaluation of technology disclosures.

TEACHING FELLOW, IVY UNIVERSITY   **2006**
Organized and led laboratory discussions and field experiments for a class of 40 students.
Prepared and graded genetics laboratory exams. Participated in Teaching Organization and Leadership seminars

PUBLICATIONS

-**Smith J**, Kevins M, DeLoite C (2008) Treatment Regimes for Glioma. *Biology Journal*, 3:22.
-**Smith J**,, DeLoite C (2005) A review of Gene Expression Analysis for Cancer. *Important Reviews*, 5:21.
-Jenkins, R, **Smith J**, Kevins M (2007) A New Gene Expression Analysis System. *Biology Journal*, 7:18.

Resume Format 3

John Smith
123 First Lane * Anytown, State, 12345 * Tel: 111-222-3333 * jsmith@email.com

Education

2007: **Ph.D.** Molecular Biology, Cell Biology, **Ivy University**
Designed statistical models of human and gene regulation. Tested 4 lead compounds to target malignant glioma. Named inventor on 2 U.S. Patent Applications.

2002: **B.S.** Microbiology, **State University**
Prepared a thesis in chemical engineering related to motif detection in DNA sequences. Further research in yeast genetics included performing experiments such as northern blots, western blots, fluorescence microscopy, NMR, PCR, drug studies in cell culture, and microbial isolation.

Other: Registered Patent Agent (U.S. Patent Office, agent's exam)

Positions Held

2011-Spring   Consultant, Start-Up Biotechnologies
 - Advised on and implemented a system to screen gene expression data for drug candidates to treat non-Hodgkin's lymphoma. Worked closely with the company founders to train scientists on the analysis system.

2009-Present   Scientist, Cancer Research Company
 - Analysis of genomic data produced by next generation sequencing platforms including full human and cancer genomic sequences.
 - Analyzed DNA and RNA from 10 skin cancer patients in an effort to identify polymorphisms that correlate with invasive cancer.

2007-2009   Intern, Ivy University Technology Transfer Office
 - Contributed research reports and summaries during venture capital due diligence. Presented marketability recommendations on several technologies to the chief of business development.
 - Organized patent filing system and assisted with the evaluation of technology disclosures.

2006   Teaching Fellow, Ivy University
 - Organized and led laboratory discussions and field experiments for a class of 40 students.
 - Prepared and graded genetics laboratory exams.
 - Participated in Teaching Organization and Leadership seminars.

Selected Publications

Smith J, Kevins M, DeLoite C (2008) Treatment Regimes for Glioma. *Biology Journal*, 3:22.

Smith J,, DeLoite C (2005) A review of Gene Expression Analysis for Cancer. *Important Reviews*, 5:21.

Jenkins, R, **Smith J**, Kevins M (2007) A New Gene Expression Analysis System. *Biology Journal*, 7:18.

Notice that the three resumes above are very similar in content but are slightly different in format. I prefer the third resume, which I feel has a cleaner look. All look very much like the formats I have used in the past, but I encourage you to browse the internet and approach your university career-services office for further examples. There are thousands of examples out there and you should choose one that best fits the position to which you are applying and the skill set that you wish to emphasize. Most importantly, your resume should have a clean, professional look. A quick glance at your resume (5 seconds) should be enough for someone to get a reasonable impression of the layout and your qualifications.

In general, I have a few very basic rules I think are important in preparing any resume:

1. The format/layout should look clean and inviting on a printed sheet. Make sure to actually print it out and *look* at the sheet before finalizing your resume. Remember that the people who read your resume will probably be looking at printed copies.

2. The resume and cover letter should be completely without spelling and grammar mistakes. If anything distracts the reader from the content, it is not a good thing for your application. Attention to detail is even more important at a law firm than in other careers. If you make spelling mistakes in your resume, your potential employer will wonder whether you will make those mistakes in court documents or patent applications. Mistakes are a huge red flag.

3. Don't use colored paper or anything other than white or slightly off-white paper to print your resume. Law firms are conservative and careful by nature, and your application should be too.

4. Show action. Many people describe their previous job duties in a resume and later include a section entitled something like "Skills." This arrangement is repetitive and takes some of the action away from your work experience. Instead, under your listed job title, describe what you did, what actions you took, and what tools you used. For example, if you worked with transgenic bacteria don't say "created mutant yeast," but rather "Employed cell culture methods, transformation techniques, and PCR analysis to create a novel knockout yeast strain." In that sentence you have described your work and also listed techniques you have mastered. It sounds more exciting and fleshes out your contribution.

5. Don't use an objective statement. In some career fields an objective statement, or "statement of purpose" in a resume is appropriate

(*e.g.*, in business or consulting it is the norm). For a scientist applying at a law firm, it is simply a waste of valuable real estate on your page. They know what you are applying for, and most interviewers will skip the statement altogether.

6. Include your GPA only if it is high. If your GPA is something to brag about (*e.g.*, 3.5 or higher), then it may look impressive to include on your resume. If not, then leave it out: the absence of a GPA won't look strange, at least initially. A firm will probably ask for this information somewhere in the interview process, but half the battle is already won if you've made it to the interview. Concentrate instead on emphasizing your experience and enthusiasm for the job.

7. Remember, this is a resume not a CV. Keep your resume to 1 page only. Many professionals with 10 or 20 years of experience still use a 1-page resume. If you truly feel that a second page is necessary, only put supplemental information on it. For instance, your second page may contain simply a list of publications and "other skills" such as whether you speak a foreign language or have a black belt in judo. Construct your second page in such a way that, if it were to be lost or if your reader forgets to look at it, your application will still be interesting enough that they will want to ask you to come in for an interview.

The comments above may be rudimentary but are nevertheless important. This list of points is clearly not comprehensive and my intention here is not to provide everything you need to know to write a good resume and cover letter. In fact, once you have a good first draft I recommend visiting a local library to pick up a few books that provide deeper instruction. Business and law school libraries usually have a particularly good selection to draw upon. Any of these sources should be appropriate as long as you keep the points discussed above in mind.

Now let's take a look at an example cover letter to get an idea of the level of professionalism that you want to convey.

Cover letter 1:

Marie Johnson, Ph.D.
77 TipTop Road,
Barrington VT, 76454

Hiring Partner
IP Law Firm
Anytown, MA

Dear Sir/Madam,

I am writing to you to submit my resume for the position of Technology Specialist with your firm. I am an enthusiastic scientist interested in pursuing a career in patent prosecution.

I am currently working as a scientist with Big Pharma Corporation where I have been the lead developer for our key prostate drug product, X44. I am responsible for directing three junior researchers in conducting animal model experiments and for liaising with upper management regarding the progress of our cancer drug pipeline.

In addition to my research activities, I have been involved in developing the patent prosecution strategy for our key drug product, the X44 inhibitor. I have worked in close collaboration with our IP counsel in the preparation of declarations to support the novelty and nonobviousness of X44. My work with patent counsel originally piqued my interest in patent law, and spurred my further research into the field. During the past year I have taken introductory courses in IP law and have completed the LSAT in preparation for law school.

The skills I have gained, both in science and patent law, make me a qualified candidate to work with inventors to prepare and prosecute patent applications as well as work with attorneys to conduct research for legal opinions. I have enclosed a resume for your review, and I will contact you within the next ten days to further discuss my qualifications. Thank you very much for your time and attention. Please feel free to contact me at the number below if there is any further information I can provide.

Kind Regards,

Marie Johnson, Ph.D.
617-716-1671
mariejohnson@mymail.com

Remember that your cover letter should be only one page long. For a law firm partner, time spent reading your application is lost billable time; in other words, a waste of resources. Three or four paragraphs are enough to get your point across, and a time-crunched attorney will appreciate a brief and effective piece of writing. I encourage you to have several people read your cover letter and provide their feedback. I have also found that simply printing out the letter and reading it on paper can give you a better perspective. While looking at the printed product you may find that the "look" or style just doesn't seem right... and those spelling mistakes seem to jump off the page. If you know any attorneys, they would be the perfect people to ask for some focused advice and proofreading.

Persistence is the Key

Winston Churchill once said "Never, never, never give up." This advice is just as pertinent to job hunting as it is in armed conflict. Because jobs in patent law are very sought after, it is important not to be discouraged in the face of rejection. Unless you are very fortunate or extraordinarily qualified, your first several (or several dozen) applications will meet with rejection. This isn't because you are a bad candidate. There are not very many positions available and a rejection may just reflect bad timing. Keep at it and never stop networking.

Below I am going to discuss several strategies you may use to reel in your first job interview. I will begin with the most basic methods (emails and "cold calls"), followed by strategies that require more time and effort: internships and informational interviews.

Emails and Cold Calls.

When you begin your job hunt, the simplest thing that comes to mind is to blindly email (or send through the regular mail) your resume to partners or human resources managers at a hundred different law firms. This is the electronic version of a cold call, where you look up someone's phone number and call him or her without an introduction. The cold email or cold call approach means firing off as many resumes as possible hoping that if enough people see your resume, at least a few will respond positively. Surely, this method allows you to get your information in front of as many people as modern technology allows. Maybe you'll get lucky, but haphazardly blasting hundreds of resumes through the web is the approach least likely to get you a response. Law firms are constantly getting streams of emails and resumes in the hope that a position is available. I once passed a printer near the HR office in a firm and noticed a stack of at least fifty rejection letters sitting in the printer tray. To my knowledge, the firm had not advertised an open position, so these were probably responses to resumes from hopeful applicants.

My suggestion is to be more directed in your job hunt and to send targeted emails tailored to firms you are highly interested in, or request informational interviews with partners at those firms. You can then use the "cold email" technique with a dozen or so other firms that you consider less interesting. In this way you focus your efforts on your "dream firm" and still get your resume in front of a few dozen HR managers.

Once you have identified your second or third tier choices and you are ready to send some "cold emails," how do you go about it? Should you omit the cover letter? Is the body of the email your cover letter? Do you submit your documents in Microsoft Word format or something else?

I recommend sending an email that briefly introduces yourself and your intentions. Your full, formal resume and cover letter should be attached as separate files in your email. Consider using something like this:

Dear Sir/Madam (remember to use a specific name if you know who the human resources manger/partner is),

I am currently a molecular biologist with Acme Co., interested in working in the field of patent law. Attached, please find my resume and cover letter submitted in application for the position of technical specialist with your firm. Please feel free to contact me at any time if you require further information. Thank you for your time and attention.

Kind Regards,
John Smith

You can experiment with this format by perhaps including one sentence describing your knowledge or background if you feel it is of particular note. For example, you may wish to point out special experience in patent law if you have worked at a firm before, if you have interned at a technology transfer office, or if you have already passed the patent bar. Also, if you are a specialist domain expert or have been working in science for many years (*e.g.*, you have 10 or 15 years experience in drug development) this might be something worth highlighting.

Conferences and Industry Events

One step up from cold calling is attending industry specific events in the hopes of networking with the right people. This is also a hit or miss approach. There are dozens of events held across the country related to patent law, so the trick is to choose the right ones to maximize your chances of meeting people in the industry who might help you land a job.

One good source of networking events is the American Intellectual Property Law Association[25], which periodically holds meetings and seminars. Another useful source is the Practicing Law Institute (PLI), which organizes courses related to all areas of law, including patent law.

The downside of such events is that they are often costly to attend and they are packed with attorneys not expecting someone to interrupt them with resumes and cover letters. My advice is to use these gatherings as opportunities to make contacts and learn about the culture of patent law rather than to hand out resumes. Once you exchange contact information with a few people, you can later follow up with a resume by mail or email. These contacts may be more likely to look at your resume after you have already met them in person.

Rather than attend large industry conferences or courses, another option is to seek out smaller, local events. It is not necessary to find events specific to patent law as long as you are reasonably sure that patent lawyers will be present. For example, in Boston the Massachusetts

---

25 http://www.aipla.org/Content/NavigationMenu/Meetings_and_Events/
Future_Meetings_Calendar/Future_Meetings_Calendar.htm

Biotechnology Council (MBC) sponsors regular committee meetings on a variety of subjects from drug discovery to law and policy. Prominent attorneys from local law firms chair the Law and Policy meetings, and most events include a networking session. Such smaller gatherings are the perfect forum for meeting attorneys and people with similar interests. Your attendance also shows that you are strongly interested in law and technology development.

Box 5-1 Other possible networking meetings

- Meetup.com: social networking site that hosts groups of people having similar interests on almost any topic. Look for groups in your area interested in patent law, tech transfer, or start-up companies.
- Biotech Tuesday (http://www.biotechtuesday.com/): gathering of attorneys, entrepreneurs, and young professionals in the biotech space. Gatherings happen in and around the Boston area.
- Mass Biotech Council (http://www.massbio.org/): Massachusetts organization promoting the biotech field. Holds meetings related to tech transfer, patent law, business development, etc.
- The American Intellectual Property Law Association (http://www.aipla.org/): holds meetings and provides educational material for patent law.

Informational Interviews

One of the most potent tools in the job-hunter's repertoire is the informational interview. Informational interviews are one-on-one meetings, usually over coffee or lunch, where you can discuss the details of a particular career with a current practitioner. These are not job interviews. They are conducted on a more informal basis, and they are usually held under the (loose) pretense that you are not presently applying for a job. The magic of the informational interview is that it takes the pressure off both you and the person you are meeting. They feel comfortable meeting you, knowing that you are not immediately expecting anything in return. In fact, they may feel flattered that you are asking them out for coffee (or lunch) just to hear about their job. The informality of your request for a casual discussion makes it more likely that a law firm partner, who may otherwise turn down meeting with a job applicant, will still agree to discuss law with you.

Don't be fooled by the informal nature of the meeting. This is your chance to make a professional first impression, establish that you are capable of doing the job, and show that you are passionate about the field. Remember that the attorney you will meet will be coming from the office and will probably be in business casual attire. You should also be dressed for the office. Wear at least a conservative shirt and tie if not a jacket, but be careful not to overdress with something like a full pinstriped suit and vest. Make sure that you also bring a folder with at least two copies of your resume and a business card if you have one.

As with any interview, do your homework in advance. Learn everything you can about the person you are meeting and their firm. What are the firm's main practice areas? Who are their primary clients? What recent patent applications have been filed by your interviewer? If you are current with such information, it will make a great first impression and no one will be able to deny that you are taking the job search seriously. You would be surprised by how many people show up for interviews unprepared.

During the course of your informational interview you should focus the conversation on what it is like to work as a patent attorney. Don't be afraid to bring up the challenges facing you as someone in the job market. Ask for advice on landing a job, but don't push for a formal interview. The person you are meeting understand your interests and will offer that interview if they have an opportunity available and if they think you are the right kind of candidate. If they don't make that offer, then just enjoy your lunch, make a new contact, and see what you can learn about the job market. Because an informational interview is less structured than a regular interview, you may ask questions that you otherwise would not. For example, you may want to know what a typical starting salary is, and what the salary progression is like... or you may ask what your interviewer feels is the most frustrating aspect of the job. Going on informational interviews does not guarantee you success, but, if you can land one, it is certainly a better way of making contacts than random networking. Always remember that sometimes job hunting boils down to who you know. Informational interviewing expands your network of personal connections.

After months of resume mailing, my first job offer was the result of an informational interview. I contacted an attorney who agreed to meet me for a discussion over lunch, and I met with him and one of his colleagues. The discussion was informal and fun; however, we did touch on my background and my reasons for being interested in law. It turned out that these two attorneys were leaving their current firm and were setting out to expand the patent practice of another, larger firm. Our discussions went on for a few weeks over e-mail, and they eventually offered me a position. I knew that there were probably better candidates out there, but I was just lucky enough to show up at exactly the right time.

Box 5-2: A note on follow-ups

Following up on meetings, whether they are casual contacts, informational interviews, or full interviews, can be just as important as making your first impressions. Lack of a follow-up is a lost contact, and possibly a lost job. At the very least it is important to send an email thanking your interviewer for meeting with you, and, if appropriate, reiterating your interest in the job. Also consider making use of social networking sites such as LinkedIn. If you have a LinkedIn profile, make sure to send an invitation to connect with your new contact.

Recruiters

Another source of help for new job hunters is recruiters. People often think of recruiters only as agents that help you seek out new jobs. Although they do hunt for job opportunities, they are also very knowledgeable in the job market and have up-to-the-minute information on practical matters such as starting salaries and benefits packages. Generally, you don't have to pay recruiters for their services. After contacting them with your information, they will decide whether they want to work with you. If they do, the next step is often to set up a meeting to discuss the goal of your job search and to review your resume. Typically, they will be paid a finders fee by the firm that eventually hires you, and so their interests are well aligned with your own, *i.e.*, to get you the highest paying job possible.

There is a certain etiquette expected when working with recruiters. Remember that they will not get paid if you take a job on your own. Therefore, once you start working with a recruiter it is important to disclose to them upfront which jobs you have already applied to and which other recruiters you have met. After all, it will look bad for them and for you if multiple people are submitting your resume for the very same job. If you are unsure about their policies, ask. Sometimes, they will prefer that you work with them exclusively.

My advice would be not to expect any recruiters to work with you if you have no experience at all. Most will not agree to represent a career-changer Ph.D. looking to get into law, but instead prefer applicants with some (even if meager) experience. Even so, you may wish to talk to them anyway. In a robust job market you may get lucky. In any case, you will at least get a feeling for which recruiting companies are active in your area and how your credentials stack up in the market. This information may be valuable later as you look for your second or third jobs years down the road.

Box 5-3:Examples of Recruiting companies

BCG Attorney Search: http://www.bcgsearch.com/
New England Legal Search:
http://www.newenglandlegalsearch.com/index.html
PremierIP: http://www.premip.com/index.aspx

A general note on email etiquette

Always remember that there is a cultural difference between working in science and working in a law firm. In a lab (especially as a graduate student) it is quite common for people to send informal emails to each other all day. Emailing becomes like an instant messenger service "Hey, check out the publication by Roberts in the latest issue of Science. –D", or "Hi, can you meet at 3?"). In law firms, as in other corporate settings, such short, informal emails are rare. Every email should have a subject line clearly explaining the purpose and context of the message. You will always address the person by name. If you are comfortable with them, something like, "Hi Stephen" could still be an appropriate opener. If not, you should always be formal ("Dear Mr. Gotz", or "Dear Stephen"). The rest of the email body should be just as formal, providing full, grammatically correct sentences.

Internships

If you have some time on your hands, the best way to set yourself ahead of the job market is to get direct experience in intellectual property or technology transfer. A great way to get started, if you are currently a student, is to meet with the administrators of your university's technology transfer office. The tech-transfer office is responsible for working with university scientists and outside attorneys to facilitate the patenting, licensing, and marketing of inventions made at the university. Accordingly, an intern can take on jobs ranging from freedom to operate searching, market research, inventor interviews, and perhaps even provisional patent drafting.

Universities vary widely on how much money they invest in tech transfer activities. Some schools retain only a few individuals tasked with educating scientists and liaising with outside attorneys. Other schools (MIT and Harvard come to mind) employ large teams of licensing experts, patent professionals, and managers to accelerate the tech transfer process. At least one (Boston University) also operates it's own private equity fund which can make direct investments in university start-ups. Some of these offices will offer formalized internship programs to which you may apply[26]. However, even if formal positions are not available, don't be afraid to inquire about volunteering for an informal internship. The contacts you can make through your university tech transfer office are often priceless, and it will be well worth the effort. Remember, these folks are very well connected to local patent attorneys, entrepreneurs, and venture capitalists.

When I became interested in patent law I was still about a year from my doctoral defense. I spoke regularly with the people at the Boston University tech transfer office and volunteered to help them with market research as needed. These sporadic projects eventually led me to work as a part-time consultant for a university start-up. While I received no compensation from any of these efforts, they provided me with important experience in tech transfer and in the patenting process. If nothing else it gave me something interesting to talk about besides my thesis when I met patent attorneys for informational and formal interviews.

Volunteering for projects with local entrepreneurs and technology transfer offices can add real substance to your resume, making you more attractive to law firms and to recruiters.

Make a Game Plan

For those of you with too much information swimming in your head, I suggest stopping at this point to write down a strategy outlining

---

26 http://www.bu.edu/otd/education/techtransferfellowships/; http://www.bu.edu/otd/education/internships/

how you will proceed with your job search. To get you started, I submit the following list of tasks in order of priority:

1. Prepare a Resume and Cover Letter. Feel free to upload your resume to websites like Monster.com and CareerBuilder. Although technical specialist jobs are not usually posted on these sites, it is a great way to get your name out there. Recruiters often review these sites, and may find your resume interesting if you tailor it properly. This is where some patent experience comes in handy because it will allow you to title your resume something like "scientist with experience in intellectual property/ patent law." Getting key words like "patent," "law," "scientist," "Ph.D.," and "intellectual property" into your resume title could potentially improve your chances of appearing in a recruiter's search results.

2. Search for conferences or local IP-related events in your area (consider whether these are feasible or affordable to attend).

3. Contact your university's tech transfer office and set up an appointment to speak with someone about official or volunteer internships. Also inquire about the possibility of working with any burgeoning companies spinning out of the university.

4. Find any classes related to technology transfer or intellectual property law offered by local universities or colleges. If you can, take a course for credit or audit a class. If you are in a Ph.D. program, keep in mind that some programs allow graduate students to take at least one course per year while they work on their thesis. Perhaps an IP course would cost you nothing with support from your department or thesis supervisor. While most law schools offer courses in patent law, don't forget to look at business schools for classes in innovation, technology transfer, technology commercialization, venture capital, or anything else related to emerging technology companies. All of these would be relevant to careers in patent law and would help you make the case to an interviewer that you are serious about entering the field.

5. Research law firms in you area. Look at web pages and attorney biographies. Make a list of attorneys or firm partners with whom you would like to speak. Make sure to keep track of their email

addresses and write some brief notes about their background and areas of specialization.

6. Spend some time on the USPTO website. Look at some patent applications and review the requirements of the patent bar exam.

7. Send out a few emails requesting informational interviews. Don't expect everyone to respond. Consider sending out 5 to 10 invitations in your first attempt.

8. After some web research, send your resume to a few recruiters that operate in your area. At this point, wait a few days or a week to see if anyone responds. You can use some downtime here to go on some informational interviews or continue your research on local law firms. Then, feel free to begin sending your resume out to law firms of interest. Make sure to tailor your resume/cover letter specifically to each firm. Don't let this process stop you from continuing to contact individuals for informational interviews.

The Formal Interview

If your efforts above have secured you a formal interview, congratulations. Half of your battle is already over. The interview process at every law firm will be different, but there are some generalizations that should be useful.

Before an interview, most firms will provide you with a schedule of people with whom you will meet on your first in-office interview. If this isn't provided, feel free to ask the HR manager for this schedule. Make sure to review the bios of the people on the list and do any other research that may be of value. As with any interview, make sure you have copies of your resume and cover letter on professional bond paper. It is a good idea to bring a writing sample if you have one available. This is another place where your volunteer work with a tech transfer office or start-up could be handy. Any memos or tech reviews you wrote may suffice as a writing sample if they are representative of your ability.

Your first interview will probably be 3 to 5 hours long and you can expect to meet with several people (attorneys, partners, patent agents, and technical specialists) for about 30-45 minutes each. If you search online for information about law firm interviews, you may find horror stories about difficult questions and tense interviews. Here you have some advantage. Because you are a scientist interviewing for an entry-level position, it will probably be understood that you have minimal experience in law. As such, you cannot be asked deep questions about legal specifics or patent filings. Instead, the interview will likely focus on "fit," *i.e.*, will you work well with their team and do you exhibit the propensity for a long-term career in law. For technical specialists, this last element is very important. Because you have no experience in law, and because paying your salary and tuition is costly, you will probably not earn a profit for the firm during your first few years. Therefore, it is critical that they are convinced that you understand what it is like to work in patent law and that you are committed to it for the long term. If you seem to be wavering or unsure, or if it appears that you are just "testing the waters" for a career in law, then you will surely lose out to a more confident candidate. This is one of the reasons that an internship or some other exposure to patent law is useful. It gives you something to talk about during your interview and allows you to demonstrate that you have had a taste of the job and that you love it.

In my opinion, the more research you do before your interview the better. Practice aloud, answering questions that you feel may come up. Have your story ready, explaining why and how you became interested in patent law. Simply explaining where you went to school and describing your thesis sounds easy, but a little practice will make your story sound much more coherent and fluid. Make sure to emphasize your interest in patent law and what you have been doing to explore the field. Did your interest spur you to take an internship or a class? Did you write an article about technology commercialization? Did you assist in writing a patent based on your work in technology? What contact have you had with the IP law community? Did you attend conferences? Now you can see how all of that groundwork you did will pay off. It shows that you are serious about the job and that you have real passion for patent law.

In your interview you should be interested and engaged, even if you are rehashing the same answers with 5 separate interviewers throughout the day. Remember to make good eye contact. If you are feeling exhausted and your gaze is wandering around the room, it may appear that you have only a lackluster interest in your interview. It is a tiring process, but it helps to be prepared by having a list of questions ready that you can ask your interviewers. This serves you in at least two ways: First, your readiness with questions demonstrates your interest in the firm. Second, the more you keep the conversation moving, the less likely it is that you will be stuck answering difficult questions. See below for a list of some possible questions you can keep in mind to ask during your interview.

Some firms will follow up the first interview by inviting you to a second round of interviews. These may be less formal, such as a lunch with some associates and partners. Depending on the firm, a second round may instead be more formal, requiring you to submit writing samples and meet with the managing partner of the office. Being invited to a second interview is great news because it means you have made it onto their shortlist of candidates. Your chances of getting the job, though not assured, are greatly improved. Always remember to stay positive, even in the face of a rejection. Interviews can be difficult and stressful. Like any difficult undertaking, your performance will improve with practice. Even if your first few interviews do not result in job offers, remember that they are valuable in improving your education and helping you get better at the job hunt.

Questions that may be asked during interviews:

➤ Tell me about your Ph.D. thesis?
➤ So how did you become interested in patent law? Interestingly, I had one attorney who was interested in what "real" work I had done in the past. It was clear that he would be happy to hear that I had held down a job doing blue-collar labor such as factory work, construction work or possibly waiting tables. In his reasoning, the ability to hold down a blue-collar job demonstrated the persistence, determination, and commitment needed to make a good attorney. It seemed that he felt that pure academicians who never held a "real" job might have more of a culture shock when moving into the legal profession.
➤ What jobs have you held in the past? Any summer jobs?
➤ Are you a good writer? (or Do you have any writing experience besides your thesis?)

➢ How much do you know about patent law?
➢ Do you know anyone else in the field of patent law?
➢ How do you feel about working in teams?
➢ How do you feel about working on a deadline?
➢ What is your strongest skill? Weakest skill?
➢ What do you expect to be your favorite aspect of patent law?
➢ What is the most challenging work you have done up to now?
➢ Have you ever faced an ethical dilemma? How did you resolve it?

Questions to ask during your interview:

➢ How is the firm organized? Is there an associates' committee?
➢ How soon do you usually allow technology specialists to have client contact?
➢ Once I complete law school, what level associate will I be?
➢ What is the firm's billable hours requirement? What is the requirement when I'm in law school?
➢ What is the mix of work like at the firm? Is it mostly prosecution, or is there a large component of opinion work or litigation?
➢ What is the most interesting opinion you have worked on recently?
➢ Do you prefer working with large companies (*e.g.*, pharmaceutical giants) or smaller start-up companies?
➢ What is your training program like? Are there formal training sessions? (Be careful with this one since many law firms have differing philosophies on the role of formal training. Some firms feel that working with clients and partners is the only meaningful training. Others emphasize a substantial seminar-style course. Your purpose in asking questions is to get information not to convey a judgment about what you feel is a better system)

Before concluding this chapter, I would like to mention some perceived biases in the hiring process. As you begin to research law firms and review the biographies of the patent agents and tech specs, you may begin to notice (at some firms) that a high proportion of hires have pedigrees from top institutions like Harvard, Princeton, Brown, and others. Although this "bias" doesn't exist everywhere (and I'm not convinced that it's more than just a *perceived* bias) you should not feel intimidated by this. It is true that some firms will only look at the very top candidates, and rumor has it that there are firms that won't consider a candidate unless they are Ivy League (read Harvard). But, you should ask yourself if you would really like to work for such a firm anyway. Certainly, academic pedigree matters, but a top performer from a state college will not be passed over in favor of a mediocre Ivy Leaguer. Stay confident in yourself and never fall prey to insecurity. Focus on your strengths and remember that you are part of a highly sought after group of professionals, trained in technology and interested in legal and social issues.

6

CHAPTER SIX

The Career Experience and the Struggle for Partnership

As you further consider your career in intellectual property, it is important to have a clear picture of the lifestyle you are going to experience. This chapter is meant to cut through the mystery and reveal what you can expect life to be like when working as a patent professional at a law firm.

To begin, let's first discuss what you can expect on your first day. For many people newly entering the workforce, the first day can be one of the most stressful in any job. This is particularly so for Ph.D. graduates who may have limited experience working outside of the university. So, what is it like?

First, it is important to emphasize that there is no typical first day, although some things are probably universal. The first person you will meet is likely to be the human resources manager who will sit down to further answer questions about salary, benefits, insurance, and other administrative matters. Soon after you will probably also meet with someone from the IT department who will explain the firm's email, internet, phone systems, and policies. Although this may sound pretty mundane, you will be surprised at how involved and complex corporate IT

79

can be. You will have to learn the calendaring features of MS Outlook, how to set up conference calls on a telephone that looks like a NASA control panel, and how to operate a corporate-style document management system. This is only the tip of the iceberg, however, because there is a host of patent related software that will be relevant to your work. For instance, every firm will employ a docketing system, software to track billable time, and probably the IPDAS software, which is crucial for managing patent related information and generating official forms and letters. Fortunately, your patent assistant should be very familiar with all of these systems and can act as your guide. Although you should learn the ins and outs of software systems like IPDAS, typically your assistant will do most of that work for you anyway.

Of course, that brings us to your office and your assistant. Yes, there is a good chance you will have your own private office and share an assistant with another associate. Getting used to working with an assistant is an important part of any attorney's practice. At first, it's a challenge to figure out exactly what you should delegate to your assistant and how to best utilize his or her skills. In the ideal case, the assistant handles all of the administrative aspects of the job (*e.g.*, preparing letters and templates, preparing assignments and Power of Attorney documents, assisting with docketing and deadline management, printing and copying, etc.). While a good assistant will handle many of these tasks, it is always important for you to check and double-check their work. As you start your new job, keep in mind that your assistant is a highly trained professional, not just a letter writer. In fact, during the first few months at a law firm, you may learn more from your assistant than from any other office colleague.

Beyond the basics outlined above, firms may differ wildly in how they handle new recruits. In some places you will experience a baptism-by-fire, where cases will be waiting on your desk the first day you arrive in the office. Deadlines will already be looming, and, without more then five minutes of instructions, you will be left to make your best attempt at preparing a response to an Office Action. This is the more stressful scenario, especially if you have never seen an Office Action before. Chances are, after a day or so of intense effort, you can produce a respectable response, though it will still need plenty of revision from an experienced attorney.

In a more guided approach, the firm may have a policy of putting new recruits through a short training period before they handle any work. The basics of patent law will be explained, and you will have a mentor to guide you through the process of reading and strategizing a response to an Office Action. In this scenario, the firm absorbs the cost of your training (as valuable billable hours are lost while you spend time learning the fundamentals). Nevertheless, the smoother introduction can be comforting to a novice.

As you may be coming to appreciate, firms will span the entire spectrum from "baptism-by-fire" to nearly spoon-feeding their new recruits. It will be difficult to know what kind of firm you have joined until you get there. Ask questions during your interview and try to gauge the culture and the state of mind of the associates. Do the associates seem happy and jovial? Are they tired and harried? Do they look bored and downtrodden or upbeat and energized? Some of these first impressions can tell you a lot about the culture of a place.

In order to give you a better feel for a typical day's work in a firm. I have prepared a few descriptions below of a day in the life of a Technology Specialist or patent agent. Based on my experiences and discussions with colleagues, I have compiled and written the stories below, and I believe that they are typical of patent practice:

Days in the Life

Day in the Life of a Technology Specialist

I wake up at around 5:15am on Wednesday. Today I want a leisurely breakfast and to watch the news before I head to work. I leave my apartment at about 7:30 to catch the subway and head into the Boston financial district.

I arrive at work at about 8:15 and check my email. We are filing a response to an Office Action later today so I review the response one more time before I send it to my assistant so that he can prepare the filing paperwork.

While my assistant is working, I review my docket and send a few emails to a partner regarding a patent application we are going to file by the end of the week. In this particular project, the provisional application has already been filed and Friday is the 12-month deadline for filing the formal U.S. utility application. As usual, the inventors waited until a few days prior to the deadline before providing us with the additional data they have generated in the last few months. This means that we have a very short amount of time to incorporate the new data, revise the claims, and get an updated draft to them, hopefully before mid-day tomorrow.

I start working on incorporating the new data so that I can give the partner an update this afternoon. At about 12pm, my assistant provides me with all of the paperwork necessary for the response to the Office Action that we are filing today. While reviewing the paperwork, I mark a few items that need further revising and also notice that we should file an Information Disclosure Statement along with our response. I provide these instructions to my assistant before going back to work on the patent application. As usual, I heat up a frozen lunch in the microwave and eat at my desk (people in our office rarely go out to lunch together as it is a waste of potentially billable time).

At 2pm the paperwork for the filing is complete to my satisfaction so I send it out to our checking department for a further review. From there it will go directly to the partner, who will approve the finished copy. At 4pm I receive a note from the partner that the final copy is ready for filing. Responses like these are filed electronically with the U.S. Patent Office, and my assistant has already uploaded the documents to the Patent Office website. After giving the electronic copy a final review, I submit the documents, authorize payment of the appropriate fees, and send out a confirmation email to the partner and client so that everyone is assured that the filing is complete.

I spend some time on the phone with another partner regarding the state of the patent application I am working on. I assure her that the draft will be ready for her to review before noon tomorrow.

At 5:30 and, although I have a bit more work to do on the application, I have to run off to class. Wednesday classes last until 8:40pm, which is early compared to the 9:40pm classes on Monday.

After class ends and I get home, I have dinner and get to bed by 11. I plan to get up a bit early tomorrow (before 5am) so that I can get a head start on the application.

Day in the Life of a Technical Specialist/Patent Agent

8:30am - Arrive at the office and check email. There is an email from a Japanese attorney asking for instructions regarding some upcoming patent prosecution in Japan. I set a reminder for myself in Outlook, and quickly review my docket for the rest of the week.

9am - I have set aside most of my day to work on a Freedom to Operate Opinion. I have finally finished the searching and reviewing of the claims in approx. 600 patent documents. That work has left me with about 50 documents that require further analysis. Today I will prepare exculpatory remarks for these patents, and flag the documents that may require more in-depth work or discussion with a partner.

11:30 - Sandwich at my desk.

4pm - Of the 50 documents originally flagged, only about twelve of them will require further work. The rest were not relevant due to claim wording, expiration date, or other considerations. For the twelve interesting documents I prepare some remarks explaining why they are potentially relevant. I will discuss these with the project Partner and he will likely ask the client for instructions before proceeding (further analysis can be quite costly if the client wants a full-blown written opinion for each document). I then forward the 12 documents to our patent paralegal, asking him to search the patent family for each one to uncover any related patents in foreign countries that we may have missed.

4-5:45 - Continue working on remarks for patents in the chart. At 5:45 I rush off to class. Tonight is Friday so class lasts until 8:10.

Another Day in the Life of a Technical Specialist

8am - Arrive at the office early to continue working on a new patent application. This technology is the first patent for a new biotech start-up, so it is a very important document. The partner is being especially thorough about making sure the writing is perfect.

12pm – Meet with the partner to review further ideas about how to structure the claims, and hear her thoughts on what else needs to be added. She asks that I prepare an updated claim set for her to review before 3pm.

12-3pm – Continue working on the claims. This claim set is very large and any changes require renumbering of the ~130 claims (and dependencies) in the claim set. Because this will be a foundational patent for a new company, we want to make sure this initial claim set covers *everything* of interest. Later, various aspects of the invention may be broken off into divisional applications, but it is important that we do a significant amount of the brainstorming now.

3pm – Send updated claims to the partner and continue working on updating the summary section of the application.

4:30pm – Meet with the partner to discuss the claims and her review of the application. She hands me a copy of the application that is heavily marked up in red ink. She asks that I have a revised version to her by morning.

5pm – I head home for supper.

8pm – 3:30am - Continue working (at home) on the application.

3:30am- 8am – I manage to get a couple hours of sleep before heading back to the office. I printed the revised application and left it on the partner's desk.

The Struggle for Partnership

Just as academics yearn for tenure, legal associates look forward to the day when they become partner at a law firm. The partner (or "shareholder" in some firms) is part owner of the firm and has a significant say in management decisions. A partner also enjoys a share of the firm's yearly profits.

As a standard of comparison, the salary surveys conducted by the NALP (National Association for Legal Career Professionals, released in 2009) indicate that median associate (J.D.) starting salaries at small and mid-size firms were about $130-$135,000 per year, while large firms (1000+ attorneys) paid a median starting salary of about $160,000/year.[27] By contrast, per partner compensation at the top ten U.S. Law firms exceeds $2M per year.[28] This clearly goes a long way in explaining the desirability of partnership.

However, just as with tenure, not everyone can become a partner. An associate will need the equivalent of between 7 and 10 years of experience to be eligible for partnership. One widespread custom is to award scientists/engineers 1 year of experience for each year served as a technical specialist or patent agent, often with the exception of the first year. Accordingly, when a scientist/agent completes law school and passes the bar exam (*i.e.*, ~4 years from your date of hire) she may

---

27 The National Association for Law Placement, Inc., "Salaries at Largest Firms Peak in 2009," http://www.nalp.org/salariesjuly09 [accessed August 1, 2011]

28 The American Lawyer, "The Am Law 100 2011 – Profits Per Partner Top 10," ALM media company, http://www.law.com/jsp/tal/PubArticleTAL.jsp?id=1202491847439 [accessed August 1, 2011]

have already accrued 3 or 4 years of experience depending on the firm's policies. Remember that the 7-10 year mark is only a lower bound, and that it may take several years before partnership is a possibility. In the end, although years of experience matter, a committee of the partners will decide whether you qualify for partnership based on a list of criteria. This list will probably include the number of hours you bill per year, your efficiency, ability to handle management decisions, ability to handle ethical decisions (*e.g.,* when dealing with difficult clients or potential conflicts of interest), and effectiveness at mentoring junior associates. When you consider all of these criteria, and the fact that there are many associates but only few open partnership positions, it becomes clear that making partner is no easy feat. It requires years of dedication, focus, sacrifice, and client service. It is not uncommon for senior associates to work well into the evening every day of the week, simply to prove that they have what it takes.

The rat race to partnership is certainly a struggle, but what if it's not for you? Are there other options? This is a good question because there are many talented attorneys who are interested in a career path with a better work/life balance. The good news is that there are several non-partner career tracks available. The first is non-equity partnership. In a non-equity position, you can be elevated to a status wherein you can make some management decisions, but you won't be shareholder of the firm nor directly share in a fraction of the profits. This position is might be thought of as a "senior associate" position, but with a nicer title, and possibly with a lower billable hours requirement. If true equity partnership is not an option, a non-equity partnership could be a good stepping-stone to full partnership at a competing firm if you can build a significant portable practice of your own.

But there are some caveats to the non-equity position. If achieving such a position is your goal, and if you can negotiate a lower hours requirement, then it could be a good career move. However, if your true goal is partnership and you are instead pigeonholed into a non-equity spot, you may find yourself working harder than ever and with little promise of advancement. The point here is to be careful and think realistically about how non-equity partners are treated at your firm.

Another parallel track to partner is Of Counsel. "Of Counsel" can mean many things, but it commonly indicates a senior position equivalent to partner in terms of respect and authority, but, like non-equity partnership, an Of Counsel will not have an ownership stake in the firm. In some firms, Of Counsel positions are identical to "non-equity" partners. In others Of Counsel may function like a part-time or reduced hours position. In such cases, an Of Counsel may not have a formal hours requirement at all. Instead of required hours and a set salary, an Of Counsel attorney may take a percentage of the hours billed-to and paid-by the client (i.e., a percentage of his or her gross profit generated). A position like this could be appropriate for someone who loves working in the law firm environment, but chooses to avoid the obligations of partnership. It is also a good position if your goal is to free up time for other pursuits like teaching or scholarly work. It should be noted that not all firms allow positions of non-equity partner or Of Counsel. Some firms may even have a more strict "up or out" policy whereby very senior associates are subtly encouraged to look for work elsewhere if they are not partnership material.

After passing the bar, some attorneys are eager to look beyond law-firm opportunities and take positions "in house." An "in house" position is a legal job with a company, rather than a law firm. More often than not, attorneys may be hired directly by one of their clients to exclusively manage the client's intellectual property work. The advantage of in-house work is that there are no billable hours requirements and an attorney will be able to focus entirely on the patent matters of one client. While an in-house attorney can become expert in a particular technology and patent portfolio, he may also be exposed to legal issues outside of the patent realm. For example, if the company is considering a merger or acquisition, patent expertise may be useful in negotiations. Or, if the company is facing a lawsuit, it is natural for its patent experts to be involved in the litigation.

Naturally, in-house positions do not usually pay as well as partnership positions, but the pay will nevertheless be excellent, the hours are typically more regular, and opportunities exist to participate in a variety of legal and business issues. As lawyers become more senior at a company, it is logical that they can also make good business leaders. Chief legal officers of a company often understand the company's strategy and business much better than anyone else save the CEO and maybe the Chief Operating Officer. If a CEO departs, a chief counsel is a natural candidate to fill the role of CEO.

Lastly, another possible path for an attorney with a few years of firm experience is academia. Lower salaries often turn people away from the academic route, but it is not often appreciated that law professors typically make more than their peers.[29] In fact, some schools pay salaries that are competitive with associate salaries. For example, a recent SALT (Society of American Law Teachers) survey noted that assistant professors at Harvard Law School are paid approximately $150,000/year.[30] Candidates who have a Ph.D. in science and a J.D. are also sought after in universities. Because such highly qualified applicants are few and far between, successful IP academics may be able to negotiate better pay packages then those in other disciplines. Yet the most significant benefit of any academic position is not money, but academic freedom. Law professors will have to teach some courses, but will otherwise be free to explore issues they find interesting. Imagine spending most of your days writing about and advocating for environmental issues, corporate governance policies, or healthcare reforms. As a law professor you would be free to delve deeply into the issues close to your heart. For anyone interested in academic law, I do want to provide a few words of caution. Graduates of top law schools dominate the professorship and assistant professor positions are extraordinarily competitive. If law teaching is where you really want to be, it makes sense to be thinking about it as early as possible. Also, be prepared for a very long process that may never be successful. I apologize for sounding glum about law teaching, but it is much more rarified and competitive than even patent law practice. For an informative and entertaining description, I suggest reading the article "The Big Rock Candy Mountain: How to Get a Job in Law Teaching" posted on the Cornell website by Brain Wendel.[31]

29 Smallwood, Scott, "Faculty Salaries Rise by 3.4%; Law Professors Still Earn Most," The Chronicle of Higher Education (March 10, 2006) http://chronicle.com/article/Faculty-Salaries-Rise-by-34-/10320
30 Levine, Raleigh H., ed. "2008-2009 SALT Salary Survey." SALT Equalizer Volume 2009, issue 1 (March 2009), http://www.saltlaw.org/userfiles/SALT_salary_survey_2009.pdf [accessed August 1, 2011]
31 Wendel, B., "The Big Rock Candy Mountain: How to Get a Job in Law Teaching," Cornell University Law School, http://ww3.lawschool.cornell.edu/faculty-pages/wendel/teaching.htm [accessed August 4th, 2011]

I hope this chapter has provided you a view of the landscape that colors life in patent practice and the path to partnership, and further illustrated that there are many exciting options for attorneys who decide (willingly or not) that partnership is not in the cards. I also hope that, as you have read more about patent law, it has become and even more exciting career option for you. However, if you are still unsure about the path you want to take, or now know for sure that law is not for you, chapter 8 will briefly outline several other alternative career tracks available to scientists and engineers. But before we get there, I want to tell you more about my experience and what happens if you try legal practice and don't like it.

7

CHAPTER SEVEN

Leaving the Law

B y now, some more investigative readers may have found out my secret. Ok, you've got me!

I worked at a law firm for two years. I completed the first year of law school. I passed the patent bar exam. Then, I abruptly went back to scientific research. At least it must have seemed abrupt to the outside observer. In your mind you must be thinking, "Why!? Why on earth would you devote so much energy to law and then take a swift exit?"

I think you deserve an explanation because it will bring to light the reasons why anyone might decide that patent law is not for them. I have also discovered that there are a number of ways that legal experience (even a short experience) can be useful in later careers. Finally, I will finish this chapter by talking about survival techniques. For many of my colleagues, and those of you who decide that law is indeed where your future lies, I will share with you the characteristics of those individuals who made a happy success of their careers in law.

A Short Story

When I left graduate school, I considered a number of career alternatives. Like any exhausted graduate student, the prospect of going back to the lab after turning in my thesis gave me a queasy feeling, very much like realizing you've just eaten a dozen spoilt oysters. But I did have a great experience in graduate school. My thesis supervisor was supportive, brilliant, and kind. My colleagues were friendly and collaborative, and I had several other mentors who were attentive and encouraging. But I was tired. I wanted to explore other options. After four years of undergraduate study and five years in a graduate program, I felt as if I was wearing blinders. I could quote cellular biology, I could explain complex mathematical methods, but I had no firsthand knowledge of how science really worked in the world... how it interacts with society. How does science impact law, ethics, business, or investment? In short, I felt incomplete, and I needed to explore other aspects of science.

So I tailored a resume and starting sending it out. My initial approach was to get my resume in front of as many eyes as possible. It was a "shotgun" style approach that many students like to try: send out 200 resumes and hopefully someone will call you for an interview. I imagined getting a hundred calls like this:

> "Is this Dr.Holloway?"
> *"Speaking."*
> "I'm with Goldman Sachs [McKinsey Consulting, the White House, <insert your favorite high-brow organization>]. We just got your resume and we would love to have someone with your expertise on staff. Would you like to come in and talk to our team? We pay six figure salaries."
> *"Well, yes. Let me see if I can fit that into my busy interview schedule."*

Well, I surely was inexperienced in the job market. Instead, I didn't get a single interview for six months. I got as far as a phone screen with a venture capital firm, and I never heard from them again.

I also had an embarrassing phone interview with a credit-rating agency that went something like this:

"So, we see that you have some experience in computer algorithms. Have you heard of the Black Scholes equation?"

"*Of course*," I said. I actually had heard of it, but had no idea how it worked.

"Great. Then tell us about it."

"*Um. Well, sure.*" I quickly brought up the Wikipedia page for Black Scholes and was met with a page of symbols that looked like hieroglyphs.

"*Those equations are very important. Yes, foundational really.* [click click click] *Extremely useful for pricing derivatives I see.* [clickity click… try to read Wikipedia quicky] *It seems that there is some integration over a series. Yes, that's about the jist of it.*"

"Thank you for your time. We'll call you if you make it to the next round."

So, after a humbling 7 months of job hunting, I decided to change strategies. I didn't know enough about mathematical finance to be competitive. But I did know biotech. And I was a good writer. I started focusing more heavily on law firms, even though I knew nothing about the law. I had already sent my resume to every firm in town. I needed a better strategy. So I started emailing partners directly, not HR managers. Sometimes I would make my email very formal, asking them to look at my resume and expressing my interest in having a job at their firm. Other times I would make my message more informal. Instead of asking for a job, I would ask only for a conversation and to buy them lunch.

This seemed to work much better. I got an interview at one firm, and landed lunch with a partner at a second. Both of these leads eventually turned into job offers, and I took a job at the smaller, boutique IP firm.

I worked for that firm for just over two years. In that time I became a patent agent by passing the USPTO bar exam, and I had the opportunity to engage in patent prosecution in the US, Europe, Israel, India, Russia, Japan, Australia… the list goes on. I also had my fair share of opinion work and venture capital due diligence for small start-up companies. This all sounds very exciting, and it was for a while.

But, there were several aspects of the job that I disliked. Firstly, I came to learn that being a scientist was too much a part of my identity.

This had nothing to do with biology *per se*, which is present by heaps at a law firm. More than anything, I missed the process of research... of being immersed in deep problems for long durations and struggling to become an expert in a specialist topic. I just couldn't think of myself as a budding attorney. Secondly, I simply never enjoyed the practice of IP law. While the theory and philosophy of the law is quite deep and interesting, I found the day-to-day practice of it to be rushed, deadline oriented, and sometimes repetitive. Some people thrive on this, and love the challenge of organizing simultaneous projects, managing clients, and meeting concrete goals. There is much strategy and intellect involved, but, like a medical doctor, an attorney must be constantly on call for their clients. They must be willing to postpone vacations, sacrifice weekends, and give up hobbies when client projects require. It was simply too much of a departure from my previous work and my academic interests. I had no real passion for it.

Working at a law firm was really a process of self-discovery. I learned that I prefer work environments with longer-term projects, few clients, exhaustive background reading, and publishable research. I gained an unbending respect for patent lawyers, but also self-knowledge that the work did not fit my personality.

When I found an opportunity to move back into science, I took it.

Secrets of Success

So I wasn't cut from the patent attorney mold. Why not, and what does it take to make it in patent law? I won't repeat the obvious sacrifices, lost weekends, or client service. Those are given, and exist in equal portions in law, consulting or finance. My question is: once you know that patent law is your passion, how do you survive the process? How do you get through law school, the patent bar, and become an associate?

I believe that the secret of success is quite straightforward: be persistent and remember to give yourself a break. In such an intense career, it's most important to stick to the basics. Work hard, rest hard, keep your goals in mind, and don't be afraid to take a break when you hit your limits. The people who I have seen succeed in this career have four essential, but common sense qualities: 1. A positive attitude, 2. excellent organizational skills, 3. great communication skills, and 4. the ability to rest when required.

No matter how hard you try, you will sometimes feel inadequate. If you are working all week, going to class at night, and studying all weekend, it is easy to feel like you can't live up to the demands of your firm and your colleagues. A positive attitude is essential. If that demoralized feeling takes over and you find yourself in a rut, your position will only become more and more dire. Those who succeed keep reminding themselves that they love the work. It may be hard, but it will be worth it in a few years. They know that the choices they make are theirs entirely, that no one has forced them into this job. Indeed, they are confident that they can make a change whenever they wish and pursue any legal job they like because they are on the right career path. They work hard, but they always keep in mind that they are working for the right reasons and that, eventually, the work will bring them greater control over their life and their career.

The second trait, organizational skills, is necessary for most jobs, but is critical in law. A large docket and a crowded class schedule will easily become overwhelming if you are disorganized. The best patent agents I have seen can bill almost seven hours in an 8-hour workday. That requires efficiency. They make detailed plans for their week, stay ahead of important deadlines, and make sure they are doing productive work each spare minute of the workday. The benefit of this diligence is the ability to leave work at a reasonable hour, the ability to free up time for studies, and the ability to go home on a Friday without the guilt of unfinished work or unreturned calls. Efficiency leads to peace of mind.

The third characteristic is good communication. This means that you can clearly convey your ideas to clients, colleagues and partners. But this isn't just about communicating project goals and timelines. Good communication also means being able to tell your partners that you are having trouble with a particular project or client, it means offering to help a fellow colleague when they are overwhelmed, and it is the ability to ask for help when things get too difficult. If you are good at discussing your problems and solutions with others it will pay huge dividends in the quality of your work and how quickly you surmount problems.

Finally, the ability to take a break is also critical. Keeping up the pace of a legal career is only possible if you can occasionally take a day (or a week) off. The most successful attorneys can recognize when it's time to take a weekend holiday or an extended vacation. Time to reflect is necessary to remind yourself why you are working so hard. Everyone needs to unwind, relax, and enjoy the fruits of their work. Without it, burnout is a real possibility.

Underlying all of these qualities is the unspoken element of passion, which I have mentioned again and again in this book. If you hate writing patent applications and you hate meeting with clients, even the most stalwart persistence will crumble eventually. My advice is that the only way to ensure that you will be successful in law is to make sure you truly love it. Talk with attorneys, set up lunch meetings, volunteer at a technology transfer office, read a few patents. Make sure that this is right for you. If law is your calling, the nothing else will matter.

What can you take from law into other careers?

Many of you might think that a two-year detour into patent law was a waste of time for me... a blip on my career ladder that needs to be explained away to all future employers. I thought the same thing, and I was prepared to be embarrassed by my 'diversion' into law and do my best to bury it in future interviews.

To my surprise, my subsequent employers have always looked on my legal experience as an asset. Because my job involved a lot of writing, they were confident that I could write clearly and effectively about science. Most importantly, the client facing work of a patent agent assured them that I would be comfortable talking with customers, leading conference calls, and managing projects by myself. On one recent interview, a prospective employer told me, "I love that you have experience in a law firm."

If you have a short foray into law, the skills you learn can be leveraged in any job whether it is business, research, consulting, or writing. Don't be afraid to try new career options. Just make sure to learn as much as you can along the way so that you can transfer those skills to your future work. It will take thought to describe all the ways by which your legal experience can be brought to bear in other fields, but, whatever job you eventually choose, you will be surprised at how well law has prepared you for further professional work.

8

CHAPTER EIGHT

Other Careers for the Technically Oriented

everal concerns often prevent young scientists from exploring a new career in patent law. Chief among them is the fear that they just won't like it. They also feel that it will be harder to move back into a scientific role after a few years away....what options will be left? Others simply fear committing to four years of evening classes and the rigors of law firm life. In this chapter I discuss career paths (other than law) that are available to scientists and engineers.

I want to encourage anyone who is truly interested in patent law to fully explore the career. If you are still interested after reading and talking to people in the field, don't let fear of leaving science stop you from pursuing a job. As I described in the last chapter, a few years spent in patent law are not wasted simply because you decide later that you don't like patent prosecution. Working at a law firm will give you valuable professional experience, acclimate you to client service, and acquaint you with the art of making presentations and conducting negotiations in a business environment. You will be further exposed to new technologies, start-up companies, and the process by which scientific inventions become marketable products. This wealth of experience can be leveraged in a number of careers outside law including policy, business management, government, or consulting. We will explore some of these intersections below.

Business Management

Scientific businesses are based on complex technologies and therefore may have equally complex business strategies. It takes a special kind of businessperson to manage projects in biotech, pharmaceutical, and engineering companies. Oftentimes, that businessperson is a former scientist. This is because they are the best equipped to have a solid grasp of the company's driving technology and therefore understand how it best fits into the business strategy.

Any scientist or engineer working in industry may eventually find himself or herself in a business position as they are promoted. It makes sense for companies to fill business positions with internal candidates, as they are already familiar with the technology, the company culture, and the organizational structure. Of course, not all technical people have the opportunity to move into a business role, and your ability to do so will be dependent on your performance in your scientific role, your sensitivity to customers and clients, and your understanding of larger business issues.

Moving gradually into a business role may take persistence and several years of patience. If you are interested in making the jump immediately, you will need a different strategy then the subtle "persistence-to-promotion" method. As a scientist, it may initially be hard to convince managers that you have any business proficiency. Furthermore, the people you are competing with for business jobs will probably be individuals with MBAs from top universities. To compete more effectively you have two options: 1) get an MBA, and/or 2) get some substantial business experience to boost your resume.

Pursuing an MBA can sometimes be a difficult decision to reach, especially because there is controversy in some circles about whether the degree has any value at all. Depending on where and how you get the degree, the MBA can actually be detrimental on your resume. For example, consider a job applicant with a Ph.D. and an MBA earned online from a little known university. In such a case it isn't clear that the person really learned anything from the education or was seriously invested in learning the science of management. Perhaps they just wanted an easy way to get another credential? Was the university accredited? These thoughts don't weigh favorably in the mind of an interviewer when the applicant is being compared to a candidate with a top-flight MBA from Harvard or Wharton. It is true that name recognition is not everything, but in the world of MBAs it holds more weight than in other fields. Make sure to be cognizant of the credentials and reputation of the school you choose.

As with any law school, accreditation is very important when choosing a business school. A reputable law school should at least be accredited by the American Bar Association (ABA) and probably the American Association of Law Schools (AALS). A vital accreditation for a business school is the AACSB (the Association to Advance Collegiate Schools of Business). Some other respected accreditation bodies are AMBA (the Association of MBAs) and EQUIS (the European Quality Improvement System), although AACSB is probably the most important in the United States. Keep this in mind as you evaluate law and business schools. Small, regional or local accreditation bodies are not as well respected nationally.

While I was vising a large pharmaceutical company in Boston, I asked a business development manager whether an MBA is a worthwhile investment for someone holding a Ph.D. He told me flat out that it was worthless if not from a top school (and in Boston this means Harvard or MIT). This was just one person's opinion, but I believe that it reflects the opinion of a nontrivial fraction of business managers, at least in the Northeast US. Despite all of this, I do not want to suggest that all evening or online MBA programs are bad choices. In the end you have to choose a program that fits into your life and your budget while effectively increasing your business acumen. Some online or evening programs are very well respected. For example Suffolk University has a well-recognized evening MBA program, and Babson has extremely prestigious evening and part-time options that may employ some web-based coursework. Just be aware that, whichever path you choose, getting an MBA will not be cheap. You should make sure that you get real value from the experience.

Also consider that classwork is not the only advantage an MBA provides. The networking opportunities of business school may be of equal importance to the instructional aspects. Fully web-based programs will offer far fewer (if any) networking opportunities. However, programs like those offered at Babson go out of their way to create good networking for part-time students. With that in mind, you should consider whether your favorite evening or online program satisfies your career goals.

If you decide not to get an MBA, and instead opt to get business experience directly, you will have to work harder in your career planning. As with other career changes, getting the first experience or the first job is often the most difficult phase of the transition. Many companies offer internships that provide such experience, but usually these are low paying or volunteer positions. If a volunteer position is not an option for you, then again consider university technology transfer offices. As mentioned previously, a tech transfer job provides experience in licensing, marketing, investment, and intellectual property. Indeed, it is quite regular for those who work in technology transfer to move directly into business development positions in science companies.

Technology transfer is, in fact, and excellent career choice in itself. There are many professionals who make lifetime careers working on tech transfer for universities, governments or other institutions. Because it requires insight into various aspects of business strategy, science, contracts, and finance, it can be a very attractive career for someone who likes to work at the intersection of science and business.

Management Consulting

Another business related career is management consulting. This field is dominated by business professionals who have MBAs from top schools. That said, I have seen scientists jump directly from graduate Ph.D. programs directly into management consulting positions with top companies like McKinsey. Many of the top firms (such as McKinsey and the Boston Consulting Group) try out cohorts of candidates during paid summer internships. At the end of the summer, they make job offers to a portion of the interns that they feel will make the best fit. The summer program is structured for MBA students who are taking the internship after their first year of business school. As such, it is assumed that their full-time job will officially start the summer following the first summer internship (*i.e.*, one academic year later). A science graduate student can take advantage of this by applying to start an internship in the summer prior to the expected graduation year. If you are lucky, you may just have a job waiting for you after your thesis is complete.

Of course, the problem with long range plans during Ph.D. studies is that they are always subject to change. Your thesis committee may require additional work, or your advisor may want you to complete additional experiments before graduation. You may also have trouble convincing your committee to allow you to take a summer off for the consulting internship when your projects are so close to completion. The best way to avoid these difficulties is to begin thinking about your long term career plan as early as possible, and include your advising professor in your discussions. Throughout your graduate studies, sit down often (much more than once or twice per year) to discuss the progress of thesis research with your supervisor, and make him or her aware of your growing interest in business. A consulting internship will come as less of a surprise to your mentor if you have discussed your interests openly with him for months or years in advance.

Of course, if you are in the workforce already, then you are not interested in an internship but a direct hire. In either case it will be important for you to show some experience or knowledge of business. Take a few business courses. Consider an MBA. Volunteer at the tech-transfer office. Do whatever it takes to build a credible business story for yourself. As a technology professional, one good way to do this is to spend some time working for (or volunteering for) a tech start-up. Even if you are doing only science, working for a start-up will expose you to all of the business problems that an emerging company faces. Because start-ups are traditionally small, you will also have a greater chance of taking on non-science responsibilities. You can then begin to build some of the experiences that will set you apart from the basic lab scientist.

During your job hunt, remember to keep in mind that there are other consulting firms out there besides the megaliths McKinsey and

BCG. In particular, there are many science-based consultancies that put a high value on candidates with Ph.D.'s and engineering degrees. Box 7-1 provides a list of just a few which you should consider.

Box 7-1- Exemplary Science Oriented Consulting Companies

Putnam - http://www.putassoc.com/ : Consulting focused on the Pharmaceutical and Biotech Industries.
Leerink Swann – http://www.leerink.com/ - Leerink is primarily an investment bank focused on healthcare and biotechnology. However, in addition to banking, they have a growing strategic advisory group that provides consulting services to high tech clients (http://www.leerink.com/services/strategic-advisory-services.aspx). Leerink also runs MEDACorp, which provides information, expert consultations, and market research to clients and to other branches of Leerink.
LEK –http://www.lek.com/ - LEK provides general management consulting but is known to have an excellent life science practice (http://www.lek.com/industries/life.cfm).
Scientia Advisors - http://www.scientiaadv.com/index.cfm - Scientia is an international firm specializing in healthcare and life science.

Venture Capital

Venture Capital funds are investment funds that contain pooled financial resources, usually of institutional investors (such as banks, pension funds, insurance companies, or university endowments), or rich individuals. VC funds are run by investment managers that direct the fund's money into companies operating in an industry where the managers have specific expertise (*e.g.*, biotech, medical devices, green technology, web 2.0). Money invested in the companies will be provided in return for an ownership stake in the company. The venture capitalist and the investors in his fund will potentially make money on their investment years later when there is an "exit" event. Such an event may be an initial public offering (*i.e.,* when the companies shares are sold on the stock market) or when the company is acquired by a larger, more established firm. Usually VC investments are considered to be of higher risk that stock market investments, because money is put into smaller firms that are developing risky, new technologies.

Venture capital has been a dream job for generations of top MBA graduates. The myths tell of endless hours of whimsical socializing and playing golf that eventually lead to the founding of hot new companies and the making of uber-millionaries. Perhaps the myth is true for some, but venture capital is not an easy profession. Few new companies are successful, and only the best venture capitalists actually make a name for themselves in the business. Unless you are one of the top managers of a VC fund, you have little chance of sharing in the direct profits of the fund's investments

A successful venture capitalist requires several characteristics. He should know his target industry like a fox knows its hunting ground. He should not only have a good grasp of the science, but he should also have a bulletproof intuition for the market. He needs to know: Who are the key players? What other funds are investing in this space? What is the growth potential? Who are the top inventors and CEOs? What is the current patent landscape? All of the foregoing information may only help the VC make the first investment. After that, he needs a vast network of contacts and associates so that he can help his new company succeed. He needs to bring in the best engineers and the top scientists in this field. If a product is delayed, he needs to know how to best stretch the invested money to give the business its best chance of success (maybe by outlasting a recession). Is the company best positioned for an IPO, or is the technology more suitable to be marketed as an acquisition target for a big pharmaceutical company?

Clearly, a good VC has a wealth of industry knowledge and experience, and, unfortunately, this is not the description of a fresh Ph.D. graduate. The truth is that you will probably need some industry experience (and maybe a lot) before you will be considered for an entry level analyst or associate post at a VC fund.

An online blog post by Seth Levine provides an excellent description of the VC job hunt (http://www.sethlevine.com/blog/archives/2005/05/how-to-become-a.php). I suggest reading that blog post twice and always remember that becoming a venture capitalist should not necessarily be a career goal, but perhaps something that you can transition into after you have thoroughly established yourself in your chosen field. It is also worth reviewing other informative VC blogs such as: http://www.askthevc.com/blog/. See Box 7-2 for other sources of VC information on the web.

Box 7-2 Venture Capital Resources on the Web

The National Venture Capital Association - http://www.nvca.org/
The Vault® Career Guide to Venture Capital – see the vault website:
http://www.vault.com/wps/portal/usa/store (search for the VC career guide).
The WetFeet® Insider Guide to Careers in Venture Capital - http://store.wetfeet.com/collections/industries-and-careers (search for the VC career guide)

I appreciate that there is a wealth of information online regarding venture capital, and most of the advice you find will be negative: "Don't bet on getting a job," or "Anticipate that you will never be a venture capitalist " are just a few of the snippets I recall from my web browsing. I won't reiterate this negativity any further. Instead, I want to point out that, despite the naysayers, there are very young people who *DO* get jobs as analysts with VC funds. These jobs are hard to get and possibly even harder to hold on to. Many of these posts are also understood to be temporary. If you have no business experience and are hired by a VC fund, it is probably expected that you will move on to get an MBA after a year or two.

There are, of course, more opportunities available if you are willing to work for free. I once spoke with a senior manager of a very prestigious VC firm in New York City, but he made it clear from the beginning that if I wanted to work with him I would have to find my own housing and completely support myself in NYC for three months during and internship. At the end of that time I would not be guaranteed a full-time job. When I mentioned that this would be impossible for me, he pointed out that he had worked for the firm for a whole year before drawing a salary. It seems that breaking into venture capital is easier if you start rich.

The point of my digressions is that you should make use of your summers while in college or graduate school if this is still an option. If you can plan for it and find a firm willing to take you, it could be worth your while to volunteer for a few months. Even if you don't get a permanent job offer, simply having a VC position on your resume may make you a more attractive candidate later (to both VCs and consulting firms), and it could certainly boost your applications to business school. As you go on the job hunt, just remember that there are few VC positions that come on the market every year, and probably less now since the start of the 2008 recession. Even with the best credentials, top grades, and a Harvard MBA, you are far from guaranteed a VC job. Considering that job hunting is so excruciatingly difficult in the VC world, I want to take a few moments now to discuss a few more things that might make anyone a more attractive candidate:

Get experience at a start-up: Any work you can do with a start-up company will be valuable in convincing VCs that you know the ups and downs associated with starting a new company. Your position is even better if the start-up is a technology company vying for, or already backed by, VC money. You can get this experience in a number of ways. Volunteer with local start-ups. Help inventors prepare pitches to VCs. Talk to people in university tech transfer offices about what new start-ups are coming onto the scene. I know that some of this sounds repetitive, but these are important items you should focus on because VCs live in the world of start-up companies. Having start-up knowledge can go a long way, not only to making you a better candidate, but also to building your confidence and maturity in the business.

Run your own blog: It seems that every young professional is starting a blog these days to talk about business or recipes or card collecting. This trend has been even stronger in the venture community where up and coming VCs describe recent business experience and post tips for entrepreneurs and other professionals. Having your own blog can give you a place to point to if someone asks about your web presence. Of course, your blog should not be filled with recipes and card collecting. Make it look professional, and only blog about business and technology topics with which you are familiar. If you can scour the web and identify local start-up companies to blog about, all the better. Your goal should be to provide company analysis and/or technology information that would actually be useful to a VC. If someone sees your blog and finds something useful, it paints you in a good light and shows that you are an active observer of the market.

Connect with Entrepreneurs: Do this any way you can. Browse the web, attend science conferences, find local entrepreneur meet-up groups (*e.g.,* look on Meetup.com). Some meetings, such as MIT's Emerging Technology conference, are excellent spots for meeting entrepreneurs and VCs. Another way to get involved with entrepreneurs on the ground floor of their business is to attend and participate in the MIT 100K competition.

Be able to analyze business case studies: When candidates interview at management consulting firms, one of the major components of the interview is the case study. This is also common in venture capital. A case interview involves your interviewer telling you about a particular business, and describing a business problem. An example scenario might be a pharmaceutical company looking to invest in the development of a new drug. They have to decide between a diabetes drug and a prostate cancer drug. Where should they put their money? Although this is much more simplified than a real case analysis, it gives you the flavor of the kinds of questions you'll have to reason through during an interview. Your ability to tackle such analysis, no matter how vague, will likely be a key component of any VC interview. Get yourself a few books on management consulting interviewing and methods for analyzing business case studies. These resources will be very valuable in helping you understand the business lingo and how managers expect you to reason through such problems.

A Shortcut to VC?

There are few short circuits in the system that may provide an abbreviated path into venture capital. One, of course, is to become a successful entrepreneur. Clearly, running a successful tech company and networking with VCs could get your foot in the door, but that strategy has it's own inherent difficulties (*i.e.,* starting a successful company!).

Another approach is through the Kauffman Fellowship. The Kauffman Fellowship is 2-year program whereby a fellow works at a sponsoring venture capital firm while also participating in a specially designed program targeted to addressing the fellow's educational needs and bolstering his network. Importantly, the fellowship is designed for individuals with little or no VC experience, making it perfect for a scientist or engineer with only a basic background in business.

The Society of Kauffman Fellows describes the program as follows:

"Each Kauffman Fellow works full-time at their sponsoring venture capital firm, which funds the Fellow's tuition. Kauffman Fellows and their firms engage in a practical, 24-month apprenticeship including professional coaching, mentoring by senior partners, and quarterly sessions of industry and leadership curriculum (totaling approximately 25 days) conducted in Palo Alto, California. As lifetime members of the Society of Kauffman Fellows, fellows and their firms join a trusted network in Silicon Valley and across 6 continents that links together hundreds of investment firms collectively deploying $50B in venture capital." [32]

---

32 The Society of Kauffman Fellows, "Kauffman Fellowship Overview," http://www.kauffmanfellows.org/overview.aspx [accessed on August 1, 2011]

Over the past several years, the Kauffman Fellowship has continued to increase in prestige. The winner of the fellowship is almost guaranteed a position in a VC firm, at least for the 2-year duration of the award. However, the fellowship actually does not pay the fellow anything. To the contrary, there is a $60,000 tuition expense covering the two years of the program (as of 2009). The VC firm that agrees to employ and educate the fellow traditionally pays the tuition and any stipend given to the fellow.

The initial review of a Kauffman Fellowship application results in the selection of semi-finalists, who undergo face-to-face interviews. One or more finalists may then be selected. If you are selected as a finalist you are considered to have met the requirements to become a fellow; however, the process is not complete until a venture firm agrees to employ you. Luckily, the Finalist will be able to use the network and resources of the program to secure introductions and interviews with various firms. The foundation also holds "Introduction Events" where Finalists are introduced to VCs, and dossiers are sent out to firms that are networked or partnered with the program. Because the Kauffman Fellows program is so well respected, a Finalist has an excellent chance of securing a position. Even better, if the Finalist does not get an offer in the first year, they may retain the status of "Finalist" for a second year.

Before you get too excited about this fellowship, make sure to review the qualifications of previous fellows and take note of how excellently qualified they are. Within the group are dozens of MBAs as well as lawyers and Ph.D.s. There are also successful entrepreneurs and people who have studied under Nobel Prize winners. Although the Kauffman Fellowship is worth exploring, it is also clearly a very competitive playing field.

The CFA is another credential that has always been prestigious in the world of finance and is now gaining greater recognition in the VC world (http://www.cfainstitute.org/). Attaining the full CFA charter is a multi-year commitment that involves three levels of exams and 48 months of work experience that must involve investment decision-making (among other requirements). If you are interested in finance more generally, but are thinking about VC in the long term, then taking the CFA exams while working in finance is a great positive step toward making yourself visible in the VC world. This credential, on top of a technology degree, provides instant credibility in the investment world.

Public Policy

A further career possibility is policy. A scientist may go into policy directly after a graduate program, after several years in industry, or possibly after attaining a law degree.

Policy work comes in many flavors but can roughly be divided into three categories: academic research, non-profit work (such as think tanks), and working for government. Policy is a very broad field and covers everything from US energy policy, the research goals of the National Institutes of Health, biohazard procedures (think CDC), and even research sponsored by interest groups that are focused on specialist areas such as health care reform or green energy. Because of this breadth, working in policy can meld elements of business, social science, philosophy, law, and the hard sciences.

Perhaps the best way to understand the available types of policy work is to review the most common fellowships offered to science graduates. Because senior positions often require policy experience, a policy fellowship is a great way to break into the field.

AAAS Science and Technology Policy Fellowships[33]

The American Associate for the Advancement of Science (AAAS) currently awards several fellowships to early and mid-career scientists each year, allowing the fellow to enter one of 4 broad classes of fellowship.

In the Congressional fellowship track, the fellows will spend their time primarily as a staff advisor for a member of congress, and/or working with congressional committees. Providing background research for and assisting in the drafting of legislation may also be primary responsibilities. In conducting their research, fellows may have to interview

---

33 http://fellowships.aaas.org/

scientists or other policy makers, and may find themselves responding to media inquiries or questions at press conferences.

A fellow placed in the Diplomacy, Security, and Development division may work within a number of specific government agencies. Although there are many possibilities, some of the most likely are the State Department, the Department of Defense, or Homeland Security. While the functions of the home agency will ultimately determine the duty of the fellow, it is safe to say that the duties may encompass anything from international charitable work to policies in trade or biodefense.

A fellow may further choose to be placed in the division of Energy, Environment, Agriculture & Natural Resources. Like the Diplomacy and Development placement, the fellow will be based in a specialist agency (*e.g.*, the Dept. of Energy or the National Science Foundation), which will determine their specific duties. Because this division encompasses several science heavy agencies, it is good choice for someone interested in the management of national scale science and engineering projects.

Finally, the Health, Education & Human Services division encompasses several agencies of special value to scientists interested in policy. Fellows here may work for the National Science Foundation, or the NIH, which commands a yearly research budget approaching $30 Billion. Since a large portion of university researchers get their funding from the NIH, it is truly a centerpiece of science policy in the United States.

In general, AAAS fellowships are probably the most widely known policy fellowships in the country, and are accordingly prestigious. You must be a U.S. citizen holding a doctoral level degree to apply. However, beyond that requirement, there are no specific age or publication requirements. The competition, however, is stiff, with applicants ranging from tenured professors and accomplished industry professionals to recent, star Ph.D. graduates.

Presidential Management Fellows Program[34]

The Presidential Management Fellowship is a very prestigious, two-year fellowship targeted at students who are in their final year of a graduate degree program (you cannot apply if you *already* have your Ph.D. or Masters degree). Beyond that, there are few formal

---

34 See https://www.pmf.gov

requirements; however, achieving the status of Finalist is quite difficult because of the prestige and desirability of the program. When the assessment (which includes a written exam) is complete and the candidate is chosen, they are called a "finalist." Finalists become "Presidential Management Fellows" only when they are appointed to work at a particular federal agency. The PMF program holds an annual job fair where finalists can interview for positions in the agencies. The range of possible placement opportunities is large and includes NASA, Homeland Security, the Securities and Exchange Commission, the National Science Foundation, the NIH, etc.[35]

Hellman Fellowship in Science and Technology Policy[36]

The Hellman Fellowship, offered by the American Academy of Arts and Sciences is designed for young Ph.D. graduates, and aims to help the fellow make a transition to a career in public policy. Hellman fellows choose to work on one of a set of ongoing agency projects related to technology policy. The projects change occasionally and are described on the Academy's website. Previous projects involved researching the funding mechanisms of science, scientists' understanding of the public, nuclear security, and educational curriculums in science. Fellows are appointed for one year, and may apply to renew their fellowship.

Robert Wood Johnson Foundation Health and Society Scholars[37]

This two-year program offered by the Robert Wood Johnson Foundation, is targeted at doctoral graduates with research experience. The program provides intensive seminar instruction and allows the scholar to spend time on policy research in collaboration with senior faculty members of a participating university. A stipend of is provided, as well as health insurance (as of 2009) as well as some funding for research activities and meeting attendance.

---

35 For participating agencies, see https://www.pmf.opm.gov/ACoords.aspx
36 http://www.amacad.org/hellman.aspx
37 http://www.healthandsocietyscholars.org/1492/1499

Others

Many other policy fellowships are available. A few of the better-known programs are listed below. In addition to those described below, I recommend visiting the following blog from Discover Magazine, which has recently been maintaining a running list of Science Policy fellowships. (The links below were all active as of 2009)

http://blogs.discovermagazine.com/intersection/2009/04/09/policy-fellowships-for-scientists-engineers/

- National Academies Christine Mirzayan Science & Technology Policy Graduate Fellowship Program *http://sites.nationalacademies.org/PGA/policyfellows/index.htm*
- National Academies Jefferson Science Fellowships *http://sites.nationalacademies.org/PGA/Jefferson/index.htm*
- Presidential Management Fellows Program *https://www.pmf.opm.gov/*
- The Robert Wood Johnson Health Policy Fellowship *http://www.healthpolicyfellows.org/fellowship.php* Note that this is separate from the Health and Society Scholars program mentioned above.
- American Physical Society Congressional Policy Fellowship *http://www.aps.org/policy/fellowships/congressional.cfm*
- American Chemical Society Policy Fellowship *http://portal.acs.org/portal/acs/corg/content?_nfpb=true&_pageLabel=PP_TRANSITIONMAIN&node_id=1291&use_sec=false&sec_url_var=region1&__uuid=2b03f683-f029-4884-8fac-27563aa4f76c*
- California Science and Technology Policy Fellowship *http://fellows.ccst.us/*

In addition to fellowships, another way to break into the field is to attain a Masters degree in Public Policy (MPP) or Public Administration (MPA). Many of the considerations I discussed above with respect to MBAs also apply to MPP degrees. Pay attention to the quality of the program you choose and consider where the graduates are going after they finish the program. Do they become consultants? Do they take business positions like an MBA, or do they end up in government or non-profit work? If it is within your budget, a formal MPP degree is an excellent stepping-stone to a policy fellowship or government position.

Note that, very much like the MBA, an MPP is largely considered a practitioner's degree. This essentially means that if you are interested in getting an academic job (presumably as an assistant or associate professor), this may not be the most relevant degree. Without a Ph.D. in policy, you will have to show a real capacity for producing publications before universities will take your candidacy seriously. That said, a masters degree is certainly sufficient for a technology person to land a private sector or government job.

If you are seriously considering public service, keep in mind that there may be loan forgiveness programs for professionals who are interested in public service careers[38]. With such a program, a significant portion of your graduate debt may be forgiven if you pursue the right job after graduation. Of course, public service jobs tend to offer lower salaries than jobs in the private sector.

Investment Banking

Although investment banking (in particular, quantitative analysis) has been popular with technically oriented graduates, the recent financial crisis has greatly impacted the number of such positions available. Because so many bankers have lost their jobs, the competition is much more fierce now than it has been in recent years. Here, I'll briefly describe some of the main investment banking divisions and how they may be compatible with a scientific background.

Investment Bank Divisions

<u>Research (Buy/Sell Side)</u> – Investment banking research is not at all like scientific research, where problems are explored to uncover new information. The term "research" in I-banking actually means the process of analyzing specific companies to forecast their performance and growth. On the "Sell Side" you will be doing such research for the sales functions of the bank, trying to forecast the performance of particular stocks and set price targets that put an appropriate value on a company.

---

38 see: http://www.finaid.org/loans/publicservice.phtml

Often you may be working with client companies preparing to offer their stock on the market. The forecasts produced in sell side research will be used to sell the stock to potential buyers. The "Buy Side" does similar research, but rather than performing analysis to sell stock, they analyze stocks in the market to make recommendations about which ones to buy. Although both sell and buy side analysis may be similar, and both may be conducted at the same bank, these departments do not communicate with one another. This separation is largely for ethical reasons, as it makes little sense to allow the seller's agents to also act as agents for a buyer. Such an arrangement would remove any incentives to make objective recommendations to clients.

You don't need a Ph.D. to do research at an investment bank, but the more quantitative your background is, the more attractive you will be to a hiring manager in I-banking research.

Quantitative Analysis – Quantitative analytics is a relatively new field in finance. Quants, as they are called, use sophisticated algorithms to price financial derivatives and other complex financial instruments. As their role has expanded, quants also devise sophisticated strategies (often called statistical arbitrage) to reduce the risk of certain investment vehicles or to optimize the amount of money made for an investment at a chosen level of risk. Some of the first quants were physicists or computer scientists, and Ph.D.'s in mathematics or statistics are highly sought after in this field. There is also a developing trend for hiring graduates that have formal degrees in quantitative finance, and many universities have begun offering such degrees in recent years. Clearly you need a very deep mathematical background to be successful as a quant. Higher-level calculus, differential equations, linear algebra, and optimization theory may all be important in quantitative analysis. Although quants will always be important, the recent financial crisis of 2008-2009 has reduced the supply of quantitative jobs. Worse, the type of statistical arbitrage and complex investments that quants helped pioneer are increasingly associated with the overly risky investments demonized as underpinning the financial crisis in the first place. Much of this stigma is undeserved, but it may contribute to a general reduction in these types of jobs in the near term.

Despite the recent economic downturn, a good quant can make several hundred thousand dollars per year. If you have a solid education in mathematics, this may be the right field for you. If you feel under qualified, consider a degree in mathematical finance or working toward a CFA certification.

Trading- There is a saying in finance that your salary is higher if your job is "closer to the money." If this is true, then perhaps it explains why traders have such high incomes, since you can't get closer to the money than when you are trading stocks. It's hard to recite an accurate average salary for people working in this category. Some can become millionaires quite quickly (or at least they did prior to 2008) while others consistently earn sizeable, but not necessarily excessive, compensation. Traders are responsible for buying and selling securities, and may come up with their own specialist formulas or strategies for picking the "right" ones. It is often described as a highly stressful job with long hours but with great rewards for those who are successful.

Operations-Operations is an excellent area in an I-bank for engineers, especially software engineers. The large number of transactions processed by a bank requires teams of specialists who understand the financial transactions and can implement them through the bank's electronic systems. Beyond simple implementation, operations personnel might be involved in managing complex data systems, maintaining financial databases, or building algorithms to more efficiently run the bank's transactions.

Other Opportunities and Closing Thoughts

As a scientist or engineer, there are numerous opportunities available to you if you are intent on a career change. Major career categories I have not covered are government intelligence (think CIA or FBI) or technical positions at government agencies such as DARPA, NASA, or the U.S. Census Bureau. To explore other options and get a deeper view of some of the careers I have mentioned in the last chapter I recommend reviewing the Wetfeet®[39] and Vault®[40] career guides which

---

39 http://store.wetfeet.com/collections/industries-and-careers
40 http://www.vault.com/wps/portal/usa/store

cover many career types from pharmaceutical research to Investment Banking, Venture Capital, and Management Consulting.

If nothing else, I hope that this book has opened your eyes to the possibilities that await you outside of the lab, particularly in intellectual property law. While you may not yet be sure that IP law is right for you, you should now feel the freedom to explore the option, knowing that the field is an interesting one, that your skills are needed, and that it isn't quite as risky you thought it would be.

Appendix A

Sources of Information on patent law and IP law careers.

The Intellectual Property Law Server
(*http://www.intelproplaw.com/Patent/*): This resource provides information on patent law and links to other useful sources. The website also provides information on careers and a forum where you can view (sometimes highly informative) user dialogues related to patent law and getting jobs in the field.

MPEP
(http://*www.uspto.gov/web/offices/pac/mpep/index.htm*) The MPEP is fully available online at the USPTO website.

USPTO (*http://www.uspto.gov/index.html*): Invaluable source of information on patent law, important case law, and the latest news from the patent world.

Patent It Yourself (*http://www.amazon.com/Patent-Yourself-David-Pressman/dp/0873375637*): This is a highly recommended book providing a how-to guide for patenting.

Brown & Michaels PC (*http://www.bpmlegal.com/index.html*) Specialist IP law firm with an excellent website providing a breadth of information on IP basics.

Patent Law Blogs: Blogs are always a great source of bleeding-edge information and the latest analyses by professors and practitioners. Some of the most popular blogs are:

Patently-O (*http://www.patentlyo.com/*) One of the leading blogs, Patently-O provides analysis and updated news everyday.

Patent Docs (*http://patentdocs.typepad.com/patent_docs/*): Focused on biotech and pharmaceutical patent information.

Patent Baristas (*http://www.patentbaristas.com/*): Biotech and pharmaceutical patent news/chat packaged in a stylish and light hearted website.

IPKat (*http://www.ipkat.com/*): General IP law blog with a focus on European and UK issues.

The Patent Prospector (*http://www.patenthawk.com/blog/*): General IP blog with informative comments on current cases.

IP Spotlight (*http://ipspotlight.com/*): Markets itself as providing information at the intersection of IP law and business.

Green Patent Blog (*http://www.greenpatentblog.com/*): As the name suggests, this blog focuses on green technology patent issues.

ABOUT THE AUTHOR

Dustin Holloway is scientist and patent agent holding a Ph.D. in Molecular Biology, Cell Biology, and Biochemistry (MCBB) from Boston University. He also holds a B.S. in microbiology from the Pennsylvania State University. Dr. Holloway is an expert in the analysis of genome data and is currently working at the Center for Cancer Computational Biology at the Dana Farber Cancer Institute in Boston.

Addendum

During the time this manuscript was being formatted for publication, the U.S. Congress passed, and the President signed into law, a Bill which will significantly remodel U.S. Patent law. Much of what I have discussed in this manuscript is still accurate, but several major changes will be enacted. This serves as a reminder to readers that patent laws, and the Rules promulgated in the C.F.R., are constantly subject to amendment and that this book is not designed or intended to be a legal reference or constitute legal advice in any way. The appropriate legal reference sources must be consulted for any true and reliable representation of the law. Rather, this book is meant to help the reader get a better idea of what it is like to work in patent law, and formulate a possible strategy for entering the legal field. It is not guaranteed to yield results or even to correctly depict what any one person's experience in law or at a law firm will be. Experiences vary, and yours may depart dramatically from the examples I have given here. I wish everyone the best of luck in their career search.

Printed in Great Britain
by Amazon